# GOOD LUCK WITH THAT THING YOU'RE DOING

*One Woman's Adventures in Dating, Plumbing and Other Full-Contact Sports*

Karen Yankosky

*For my family*
*You are my everything.*

# TABLE OF CONTENTS

# PREFACE

This collection of humor essays takes you on a scenic drive through my life as a 40-something who's reinventing after a marriage even Hollywood would call brief. Many of these anecdotes appeared first in some form on www.splatospheric.com, the humor blog I started in July of 2012 after that whole marriage "oopsie."

These pieces involve real people, real events, and real sarcasm, though I have changed names and other identifying details where necessary to preserve anonymity. The views expressed here are mine alone, and I tell it like I see it.

I hope you enjoy the ride, and apologies in advance for my lousy sense of direction.

# 1

---

## BECAUSE INTRODUCTIONS ARE FOR SISSIES, AND NO ONE READS 'EM ANYWAY

---

My family, like most, has a bunch of running jokes. My father generated one of our all-time greats just before I took the Virginia bar exam in the summer of 2002.

My classmates and I had started to prepare for the test right after graduation because we had only six weeks to absorb a staggering amount of material. With each day that passed, my stress level began to rise slowly but steadily, like the sea level. I tried to ignore it but my subconscious wouldn't let me. To make sure I was paying attention, it introduced a recurring dream involving my car and a fictional pothole on my parents' street in Northern Virginia.

The first time I had the dream, I was driving my red Honda Civic past my childhood home in Springfield, Virginia, when I encountered a slight dip in the pavement. The sedan and I glided right over it. As I continued to have the dream, the pothole grew wider and deeper. Soon, my stalwart Civic struggled to cross it and began to sacrifice parts along the way. I awoke each time feeling somewhat amused and also slightly disturbed.

I mentioned the dream in passing to my parents, and they didn't find it funny at all. They immediately offered to help and suggested that I study at their house for a few hours every day. They even promised to feed me while I was there. (If left to my own devices, I would have subsisted on a diet of Brown Sugar Cinnamon Pop-Tarts with the occasional bowl of Cap'n Crunch thrown in for variety, and they knew it.) Though I was thirty-one and had been living on my own for years, I accepted their offer.

Mom and Dad went a step further with their generosity and even helped me study. The two of them took turns calling out questions from the flashcards I had prepared, which, if stacked end-to-end, could have made four complete loops around the Beltway. Mom and Dad had a surprisingly high tolerance for my recitations of obscure points of law, but the same could not be said for my penmanship. It drove my father especially crazy. Dad would pick up a card, squint, hold it out at arms' length, bring it back to within millimeters of his nose, and then finally guess at its contents.

He once pulled out a card and, after studying it, said, "Explain the 'rude aghast palpitations.'" I snickered.

"Oh, you mean the 'rule against perpetuities,' Dad." I braced myself for a three-Hell response.

"Well how the Hell was I supposed to know what the Hell that was? And what the Hell happened to your handwriting? Maybe you should take the medical boards instead of the bar." Comic relief like this helped keep me sane, even as the pothole of my dreams had expanded to the point where it claimed my car's muffler and exploded a tire.

On July 28, 2002, I got into my Civic and drove 238 miles to Roanoke, site of the bar exam, a gigantic hilltop star, and, well, that's about it. I slept fitfully in a hotel room near the exam venue, waking up hours before my alarm went off and moments before the pothole swallowed my car completely. I had promised Mom and Dad I would call them before the test to get a last-minute infusion of moral support. I reached Mom at home, where she was relaxing and enjoying the summer off from her job as an elementary school librarian.

She played her part perfectly and said all the encouraging things Moms are supposed to say, like, "You've worked so hard, honey," "you're ready for this," and, "don't worry, you're going to do great." With the Mom endorsement locked up, I moved on to Dad. My father had come out of retirement to work part-time for a defense agency and spent most of his day doing classified stuff in a locked-down office. I almost never interrupted him there, but he had assured me it was okay to call him at the office that day. I dialed.

"Yank, here," he said. It was his standard greeting, but his tone was gruff. I wondered if I had caught him at a bad time.

"It's me, Dad."

"Uh-huh," he said. Not exactly the response I expected.

"Um, well, the test starts pretty soon..."

"Yep." I waited for him to say more, but nothing else came. It hadn't been a pep talk so much as a pep syllable. It figured that the one time I actually craved a lecture from my father, he gave me a lesson in efficiency instead.

"You, ah, well, you told me to call you right before I went in. Remember?"

"I do."

"And...I think you wanted to tell me something?"

"That's right."

"Go ahead, Dad, I'm ready." As I waited for the font of fatherly wisdom to start flowing, it hit me: maybe my father couldn't muster up more than a few words because the idea of sending his baby girl off to become a lawyer had him all choked up. How could I have been so blind?

Just as I was envisioning Dad having a Moment, fighting to stiffen his upper lip, he cleared his throat and said, "Good luck with that thing you're doing."

Good luck with that thing I was doing? Huh? The bar exam I'd spent four years in law school and six weeks studying for, the test that made me dream of car-swallowing potholes, was "that thing"? I hung up and called my sister Lynne. When I told her what happened, she laughed so hard she couldn't form a complete sentence.

"'Good luck with that thing...?' Hahahaha!" I sat back and let her laugh. "No really, let me get this straight. He really said 'Good luck with that thing you're doing'?" She was teetering on the edge of hysterics. I pictured her dabbing at her eyes, a visual that took me exactly where I needed to go.

When Lynne and I were kids, we sat across from each other at the dinner table every night. It was the only spot in the house where we didn't fight. Almost without fail, something would happen during the meal that would make one of us start giggling—usually something only the two of us found funny—and the other would follow, resulting in a crack-up relay.

My father always tried to end it by mock-yelling, "Quit your damned cackling!" Which, of course, fueled at least one more lap around the laugh track. By sending my mind back to such a familiar and welcome scene, my sister had set me up perfectly. I walked into the Virginia Bar Exam fighting off a major case of the giggles.

Pretty soon, "good luck with that thing you're doing" became a verbal talisman for our whole family, wielded at only the most absurd times. Headed to the dentist for a root canal? Got an overflowing toilet? "Good luck with that thing you're doing," we'd say and always get at least a chuckle in return, no matter how lousy the situation.

A decade after the bar exam, my siblings and I were trading somber emails about our plans to drive to Pennsylvania to visit our 91 year-old grandmother. Nana's health had begun to deteriorate quickly. She had endured more than her share of suffering, but that didn't make it any easier for us to accept that our time with her was running out. My sisters wrote to say they'd decided to drive up to see Nana that day. Thanks to Dad, I didn't have to think very hard to come up with the right words for the occasion.

"Good luck with that thing you're doing," I wrote.

# 2

## YOU'VE BEEN SERVED

Divorce is a hideous experience, even if you're the one who wants it, but at least it encourages reinvention. You can make a fresh start in all kinds of ways: change your name, overhaul your wardrobe, or do what I did and take up amateur tennis.

My mother recruited me to join the Smash Hits, the women's tennis team she'd been playing on for years, at the perfect time: when I was smack in the middle of a move. The phone rang one evening in the spring of 2012 while I was surveying the wreckage that covered the floor in the guest room of my new house. This room had become a dumping ground for containers unloaded by movers who, in a bold departure from centuries of relocation precedent, had shown up at my old place three hours ahead of schedule. Few people would call me "organized" on my best day, and exactly zero would call me that on a day when I'd been thrust into a packing emergency. I hurled my possessions into any empty box I could find, barely able to maintain a one-box lead, much less pause for niceties like labeling.

As excited as I felt to be in the new house and to leave my disastrous ten-month marriage behind, solving the Mysteries of the Boxes enthralled me less. I was desperate for a diversion and therefore an ideal target for Mom's pitch. (I would have been an easy mark for anybody's pitch. Had Time-Life Music called instead of Mom, I would now be the proud owner of the "Beloved Funeral Hits" collection, no doubt.) The Smash Hits, Mom explained, were getting a bit long in the tooth. The league the team played in had set the age hurdle at eighteen years, and the average Smash Hit cleared it with four decades to spare. The team needed more players, and younger ones.

I mulled it over. Why not make "tennis player" part of my new identity? I liked the idea that somewhere out there a group of people existed who viewed forty-something athletes as young. The fact that I hadn't played the sport in a meaningful way since my days on the Fox Hunt Junior Tennis Team in the summer of 1984 didn't faze me. Back in those days, tennis, like me, did not exactly have a high cool quotient among teenaged girls. This made for slim pickings in the fourteen and under age group and landed me at the number one singles spot. I enjoyed playing but didn't take it seriously. The competition did, however, and soon left me behind. The prospect of getting back in the game twenty-seven years later held enormous appeal.

"Count me in, Mom," I said. My mother, not at all the girly type, let out an uncharacteristic squeal of delight. I felt a bit giddy too. When I was a kid, Mom had been actively involved in all the sports I played –she even coached my soccer teams—but we'd never been given a chance to compete together.

Unbeknownst to me, my return to the courts had caused a deep divide (and some split sides) within the rest of my family. Dad, along with my sister Lynne, voiced some skepticism, probably because they remembered my tennis career. My brother, L.J., chose optimism over history and expressed nothing but confidence. My oldest sister, Suzi, abstained. (Suzi never has enjoyed a good old-fashioned pot-stirring quite as much as the rest of us.) To prevent the debate about my skills from raging out of control, my family settled it by using a trusted dispute resolution tool: they bet on it.

I discovered this after the first practice outing with my father, when I overheard him say to Lynne, "She didn't stink up the joint anywhere near as badly as I thought she would. Looks like I owe your brother ten bucks."

Dad was right: my game seemed to have more pluses than minuses. My running habits kept me relatively fit and allowed me to cover the court well. I also used every square inch of the racquet, whereas your less versatile players tended to limit themselves to the strings. Because so many of my shots emanated from the frame, they landed in ways even a gifted physics student would have struggled to predict. On the downside, my serve had all the consistency of Charlie Sheen in his "winning" phase.

"Don't worry about your serve," Mom said. "You're just getting started. You'll get the hang of it again in no time."

The Smash Hits' first match was scheduled to take place fourteen days after my mother's call and gave me little time to refine my game. Our team captain, a believer in the tennis version of the Hippocratic Oath, placed me at the spot in the lineup where I could do the least harm—number three doubles—and paired me with Mom. That didn't bother me. The fact that I had peaked athletically at age eleven didn't dampen my competitive spirit, either. Just before taking the courts at the Army Navy Country Club in Arlington, a venue that would deny me admission under any other circumstances, I reminded my partner that I don't like to lose.

Mom nodded and then, as proof of her killer instincts, said, "Did you notice how much cuter our outfits are?" I made a mental note to have DNA testing done after the match.

Mom and I took the court against two women who looked to be quite fit and roughly my age. I watched them during warm-up and saw enough to know that we were going to be in for an epic battle, assuming one can battle epically while wearing a ruffled skirt. Sixty minutes into the match, Mom and I brought the first set to a tiebreak and won it, a development that surprised us only slightly less than our opponents. We compensated for it with an efficient choke in the second set, losing four games straight in half the time it took us to win the entire first set.

Our second set deterioration stemmed in large part from my serve. I had begun to experiment with putting my whole body into it. When I did that, I achieved an instant increase in speed and power, but it was offset by a loss of directional control. The convergence of these forces caused me to send my partner a strong, nonverbal hint to start parting her hair on the left. With the next serve I disproved that old chestnut about mothers having eyes in the back of their heads because, if Mom had had them, she wouldn't have gotten beaned.

On witnessing the moment of impact, our opponents' hands flew to their mouths and they gasped in perfect unison.

"Oh my God, Mom, I'm so sorry!" I said as I dropped my racquet and ran over to her. She looked all right, if slightly stunned.

"You hit your *mother*?" one of our opponents said. I nodded, triggering a fresh round of synchronized gasping. At least I hadn't hit Mom hard enough to draw blood, though under the league rules, that would have entitled us to an injury time-out. We had to resume play before I even got to ask my mother if she planned to write me out of her will.

I somehow managed to locate my self-discipline and bring my serve under control. Mom's play got better too, because having to fend off both your partner and your opponents tends to improve your reflexes. We managed to win a game and had brought the next one to deuce when the buzzer rang to end the match. We hadn't finished the second set, but under the league rules, it counted anyway because the other team had won four games and was ahead of us by more than two. With the match tied at one set apiece, our fate rested on math. Our opponents had won more games in total than we did and were declared the winners. Despite the outcome, I was proud of myself for summoning up the guts to get back out there, and I loved playing with Mom.

My father called me at work the next day, wanting to hear my take on the match.

"Well, I wish we'd won, Dad, but I still think it went pretty darned well."

"Yep, your mother thought so too."

"I'm so glad to hear that," I said.

I was also relieved, because Dad hadn't said a word about the fact that I'd smashed that errant serve right into the back of Mom's skull. The unfortunate accident was precisely the kind of thing that would become a staple of Yankosky folklore. Family members would tell and retell the story, embellishing it over time until one day I would hear my brother say, "And then your aunt loaded the tennis ball into a bazooka. That's right, kids, she shot a tennis ball at your grandmother's head with a bazooka." Surely Mom knew this episode could easily take on a life of its own if she spilled the beans. I could only hope that her trademark selflessness would come to my rescue and keep my blunder from becoming family legend.

"Did she say anything else, Dad?"

"No, I think that was about it." I exhaled loudly. "Oh wait, now that you mention it, she did ask me to shave the back of her head and look for a 'Penn' tattoo." He snickered.

Aside from having made yet another dubious contribution to our family anthology, I rather liked the way my fresh start was shaping up, including my return to tennis. If all great inventions involve disruption, maybe all great reinventions involve concussion.

# 3

## AN UPHILL BATTLE

I used to like riding my bike before I married a ridiculously fit, hill-loving cyclist. Early in our courtship, my future ex-husband and I tried to make biking an "us" activity. Spending time doing together something each of us enjoyed individually made great sense as a concept, and it worked well at first. But I was the weaker cyclist by far, and after a while I could tell he was getting tired of slowing his pace for me. I couldn't blame him. I had a better chance of melting a glacier by breathing on it than catching up to him on the bike. As time wore on, we continued to ride together, by which I mean we pedaled in the same time zone. Eventually our joint rides made me feel like I was in the Tour de France, chasing a fully juiced Lance Armstrong while mounted on a Big Wheel. Frustration replaced fun and fulfillment (and in that way paralleled the trajectory of the relationship). When I decided to end my marriage in July of 2011, I severed my ties with cycling, too, and I didn't miss it.

Getting divorced freed me of all kinds of baggage and allowed me to let go of some of my loathing for the bike. Since I had moved to a neighborhood that had access to three trails within a half-mile of my front door, it seemed crazy not to at least give the pedals another shot. The idea of getting back on the bike produced some of the same anxieties that surface every time I've considered rekindling an old relationship. Would I be welcomed back, no questions asked, and return immediately to the status I held before the hiatus? Or would I have to endure a round or two of punishment first? I decided to confront those questions on a hot July morning before work. With no meetings scheduled until 10 a.m., I had enough time to fit in a ride of decent length.

This being a typical summer day in Washington, D.C., I should have just spent a few more months with my head stuck in the sand, because the air quality would have been better there. Casting aside common sense and warnings about red air, I got on my bike, pressed the soles of my shoes into the pedals, and waited for the metallic click that would let me know my feet were locked in. My ex-husband had outfitted my bike with the clip-in pedals shortly after we met. They were supposed to make me ride more efficiently, but the only thing they seemed to improve was my talent for slapstick.

On clipping in, I made my way to the entrance of Arlington's Custis Trail, a path leading to a trail that hugs the Potomac River. I'd planned to ride along the river to National Airport and back, a round trip of roughly seventeen miles. As I approached the airport, my legs still felt fresh, so I sailed right past it and cycled another couple of miles to Belle Haven Marina. There, I began to look for a spot that would meet my stringent criteria for turning around, namely soft vegetation in case I couldn't dislodge my shoes from the pedals. (Having made more than my fair share of unsuccessful attempts to unclip, I'd become quite the connoisseur of shrubbery.) After I about-faced, it took mere moments for me to realize I'd attributed the freshness of my legs on the front half of the trip to the wrong cause. It wasn't my extraordinary level of fitness; it was gravity. The ride to the marina had been almost entirely downhill, even the seemingly flat parts of it.

The prospect of riding ten miles uphill in increasingly hot and un-breathable air leeched the motivation right out of me. The imminence of that ten o'clock meeting kept me on the bike, but I was pedaling no faster than teeth shift. Traffic on the path was minimal, allowing me to focus completely on my misery. I was so busy wallowing in it that I nearly toppled over when a rider behind me called out, "Passing, left!" As I shifted to the far right, I was overtaken by a beefy guy riding a bike that looked like Dorothy's from *The Wizard of Oz* and sounded like it came off the same assembly line that produced Chitty Chitty Bang Bang.

Talk about demoralizing. It reminded me, not in a good way, of the first sprint triathlon I did in 2005. I had exited the swim in a very respectable second place. Knowing that I wasn't the strongest cyclist— at the time I didn't even own a bike and had borrowed one for the race—I did not expect to hold that position for long, and my expectations proved accurate. I was left in the dust immediately by some stunt doubles from *Breaking Away*. Less than a mile later, the world's most mediocre peloton (French for "two-wheeled clump") whizzed past me, and I quit trying to keep track of my standing in the field. I knew I had no chance at placing, much less winning, yet I was still completely unprepared to be passed halfway through the ride by a profoundly potbellied competitor whose entire racing uniform consisted of a pair of Nikes, white ankle socks, and an overworked, low-coverage Speedo. I don't know whose efforts I respected more, his or the bathing suit's.

As the triathlon incident proves, I'm no stranger to cycling-related humiliation, so I'm not about to give up. The bike may have let me know in no uncertain terms that I have quite a ways to go before it's ready to start speaking to me again, but at least I broke the ice.

# 4

## GET IN THE GAME

Last week, Groupon advertised a deal from a company that specializes in personalized matchmaking. For a mere $65, Washington-area singles could buy a month of the company's expertise in arranging targeted introductions. I deleted the offer, thinking I didn't need it, but on mentally reviewing my relationship resume, I began to wonder whether I had dumped it too soon. The entries from 1996 to 2009 revealed a tendency to pursue men whose availability varied inversely with their charisma. The 2009 2011 segment included a marriage of such misery and brevity that I couldn't even call it a starter marriage. It was a non-starter. For the year or so that followed, I had been sitting on the sidelines of dating, essentially on injured reserve. Yet this status hadn't been enough to shield me from an ugly crash months earlier with a player who stepped out of bounds and kept running even after he collided with the bench.

I had made plans to meet my friend Meredith for dinner at a nice Italian restaurant in Fairfax, the Northern Virginia suburb where she lived. My dinner plans were preceded by an always-dreaded hair appointment. The haircut took far less time than usual (and the stylist produced superhuman results), so I found myself with forty-five minutes of unexpected free time. I decided to go to the restaurant early, grab a seat at the bar, and start reading a guidebook I'd bought in preparation for an upcoming trip to Germany. The restaurant's rectangular bar had four empty seats in a row. I made a beeline for that section, grabbed the stool farthest from other patrons, and opened my guidebook. I hadn't even reached Berlin in the table of contents when I felt a tap on my shoulder.

"Excuse me, can I sit here?" asked a man of average height and build with thick, silvering hair and blue-green eyes. He pointed at the stool right next to me. He was handsome, but attractive or not, I didn't want a neighbor just then. Still, I felt I had no right to say no, so I simply nodded.

"I'm Rob," he said with a smile. He seemed nice, as much as you can read niceness from looks alone.

Perhaps because of that I made the rookie mistake of introducing myself using my actual first name. I realized my blunder and tried to mitigate the damage by returning my full attention to the guidebook. I felt certain this gesture would cut off the conversational airway.

Rob forced it back open with a quintessentially Washingtonian chestnut: "So what do you do?"

Something about the way he was looking at me set off my Creep-O-Meter. I should have said, "I'm a sprinter" and made a run for it. But instead of heeding my instincts, I went on auto-polite. I answered truthfully and told him that I practice law. Rob volunteered that he worked in construction and does windows and siding. He thrust a business card in my direction. On realizing he might just be trying to sell me some vinyl, I felt a brief euphoria that I hoped didn't register on my face. I took the card even though I didn't need vinyl, windows, or anything else from this guy. He continued to talk, making it clear that he wanted to sell me something more than siding. I tried again to kill the conversation, this time with expectant glances cast alternately in the direction of the door and my phone, which sat on the bar. He asked me for a card. I claimed not to have one on me, which was true if you used the most literal definition of "on." None of it fazed him.

"Well, I see you have a phone," he said, "so why don't you just text me your number?" Had I not been out of the game for so long, I might have seen that one coming.

"Oh, sorry. I'm actually still married," I said, glad that my marriage had finally been good for something. I felt certain this would finish off our chat, but my comment spawned more questions than a Maury Povich interview.

I explained that I separated from my husband after less than a year of marriage and that I had taken up residence in my sister's basement. Being still-married and living in a family member's basement is widely recognized as a solid, two-pronged defense against suitors. It should have worked at least as well as the time when my sister and I were at a crowded bar and she decided to broadcast her belief that she might be coming down with pink eye. But my revelations had no impact on Rob, who didn't relent. Eventually I ran out of steam and gave him my number, thinking I was making a bigger deal of it by continuing to stonewall. He entered the numbers into his phone and called me as I stood there. Clearly he was no rookie. Then he said he liked my "look." While silently cursing my stylist, I pointed out that I almost never looked that way. (This was true. I had a better chance of painting a perfect replica of the Sistine Chapel ceiling than recreating my stylist's work.)

Those comments somehow came across to Rob as an invitation to show me every photo he'd ever taken on his cell phone. The first several were of his English bulldog, Winston. My face must have conveyed disinterest in Winston, because Rob switched from pictures of live animals to snapshots of cooked ones. The screen of his phone was suddenly occupied by a veritable field of scored chicken parts arrayed on a grill, and then by a photo of the seared veal chop he'd ordered at a restaurant weeks earlier. Unless you're a restaurant critic or doing an exposé on animal cruelty for *60 Minutes*, I really don't care about your food photos. I was about to say as much when I saw Meredith walk through the door. I forced out a "nice chat" instead and rushed off to meet her.

Ten minutes later Rob materialized at our table. Since I couldn't ask the server to do something about the barfly in our soup, I instead dropped a bunch of hints that Meredith and I wanted to be left alone. When one of those finally found its mark, he walked away. But apparently Rob still hadn't been ready to let the conversation die, because a post-dinner glance at my phone showed that he'd texted me seven times over the course of an hour.

I perused the messages in order. The first four were benign and banal, standard "nice to meet you, hope to see you again" fare. The fifth asked whether I was wearing a thong, and if so, what color. In the sixth he wondered if he'd done something to offend me. With number seven he said I had issues and noted that it was a shame because he'd been hoping to take me to his favorite place. Based on the meat photos, I had to assume he was referring to his freezer. It wasn't a stretch to imagine myself chopped up and ziplocked in there, right next to the pork loin.

That experience sent me running off the field and straight for the locker room, where I've been hiding ever since. But I think I'm ready to suit up again and make a coaching change. For $65, it could very well be worth it to find out whether a paid professional can mismanage my dating life as expertly as I have.

# 5

## PUT YOUR MONEY WHERE YOUR MOUTH IS

I got married on October 2, 2010. When the day that was supposed to be my second wedding anniversary rolled around, I couldn't help but reflect on my defunct marriage. It hadn't lasted long enough even to have a first anniversary, so October 2, 2012, was really the first anniversary of our not having a first anniversary. I had no specific plans for the date, yet somehow it turned out perfectly. Perfectly awful, that is.

After I started the day off in the calendar hole, Mother Nature got into the act and flooded the hole with torrential rain that lasted most of the day. (My actual wedding day, by contrast, featured cloudless blue skies and temperatures in the seventies. I should've known it was a very bad omen. When I think of marriages that have gone the distance, most of them involved nuptials that were marred by rain or some other mishap. My parents, for example, have been married for more than 45 years despite the fact that, during my mother's bridal shower, a homicide was committed right next door. Mom and her friends were oblivious, of course, because things get pretty wild any time a group of women chug fruit punch and dress each other up in toilet paper wedding gowns.)

Rainy days can be great when timed well, but this one wasn't, because it was interfering with my lawn. I had recently hired a service to save my ailing yard, and they used a multiphase approach (as your better rehab programs do). Phase one, which they had finished two weeks earlier, consisted of killing the weeds. In my case, this meant killing the yard itself, giving me the only albino lawn on the street.

Phase two entailed reseeding the whole lawn. The service finished that on October 1, roughly sixteen hours before the un-niversary rains began. The street I live on slopes steeply and my house sits toward the bottom of the hill. Any time we get a deluge, the water rushes downhill and goes tearing through my backyard before it ends in a pool who knows where. Based on the biblical downpours we got that day, I didn't retain a single seed, but some downstream homeowner will be thrilled to wake up one day to an inexplicably verdant lawn.

At 2:00 p.m., I went to the periodontist for a follow-up appointment. It turns out that recession didn't hit just the auto industry: it had gotten my gums, too. I purposely scheduled the follow-up appointment for a Tuesday because experience had taught me that the news probably wouldn't be good no matter when I got it. Dental professionals have spent decades assaulting my mouth, and not one of them has ever burst into the room and said, "This one's on the house!"

When I had the initial consultation two weeks earlier, the periodontist took a few moments to review my X-rays, patted my shoulder, and said, "I'm confident I can help you," by which he meant, "I'm going to Bali."

At the follow-up appointment, the doctor took me through an eighteen-slide, thirty-minute presentation on the anatomy of teeth and gums. Due to the recession of my gums, the doctor explained, the bones of my teeth had shifted and were starting to sink, like Venice. Periodontists combat this by constructing a wall of sandbags in the patient's mouth.

I'm kidding. A mouth lined with two feet of grit would be infinitely preferable to the actual remedy, a charming procedure known as "gum grafting." This is a form of oral surgery in which the periodontist scrapes skin from your palate and sticks it onto your gums to fortify them. Without this boost to your gums, your teeth would be like the top of an unstable cheerleading formation: they'll manage to stand up, but they might be a bit wobbly, and sooner or later they'll topple over.

After he explained this in slightly more technical terms, he summed up by saying, "The good news is you don't have periodontal disease." Dentists love to inform patients using the good news/bad news format, so I knew where he was headed next. "The bad news is you do have 'patient's disease.'" I'd somehow gone overboard in taking care of my teeth, he told me. He let out a little chortle. I found no humor in what he was telling me, but I did locate a very strong urge to rearrange his gums.

I pointed out that I used an electric toothbrush, like the experts say you should. True, he said, but it was the wrong kind of electric toothbrush for my tooth structure. Of course. I must've missed it when they covered that in law school. And my habit of flossing two times a day was too religious. Apparently I should've been on a more agnostic frequency. The cost of my hygienic overzealousness and weak dental genes? $2,500 per graft, and I would need three.

"How much are dentures?" I asked.

I could do a lot with $7,500, such as buy first-class plane fare to Italy, where my mouth could decompose amid picturesque scenery. But because I'm single and know that the dating world places a premium on having certain original equipment, like teeth, I decided to do the grafting instead of going on a few nice vacations. Let's face it: $2,500 might be a lot to pay for a piece of gum, but it beats buying an anniversary present.

I had the first graft done two weeks later. A technician took me back to the room to get things started and then the doctor came in to prepare the local anesthetic. As he pulled back the needle to administer the first shot, he said, "This will feel like a very short pinprick." I grunted to signal my understanding. Before he administered the second, he said, "This one'll sting more. It'll feel kind of like a bad splinter."

I don't know why he felt the need to forecast my level of discomfort as if it were the weather. Perhaps he just wanted to make sure I had the right amount of trepidation going in to each shot. After all, you don't want to get caught with a mere "affectionate pinch" level of dread in a situation that requires something more like "convenience store stabbing."

When he finished, he said, "Just to let you know, I also numbed the adjacent areas. You don't want the neighbors to get upset about the party next door. Heh-heh." I don't know about you, but if I get wind of my neighbors throwing a party that involves palate scraping, I'm calling the cops. After a few minutes the numbing agent did its job, leaving the periodontist to do his. He resumed the play-by-play, which remained as informative as it was unwelcome.

As I heard the sound of metal against tooth, he said, "What I'm doing right now is not unlike some things a hygienist does. So think of me as a hygienist with a really deep voice." I could tell he'd delivered this punch line before and thought it crushed. Perhaps he failed to realize that an audience consisting entirely of open-mouthed hostages tends to be restrained in its criticism.

"Now I'm going to borrow some cells from your palate." He made it sound benign, like a library transaction. Based on the explanation he'd given during the initial consultation, I knew this deal was more like loaning money to a relative: once it left, you'd never see it again. My palate understood this too and seemed reluctant to bid the tissue farewell. My eyes tracked the doctor's hand as he moved a metal instrument back and forth in small strokes across the roof of my mouth, the way you'd use a butter knife to scrape char from a piece of burnt toast. I detected the singular metallic flavor of blood and began to wish the anesthesia had numbed my taste buds, too.

An hour and a half and $2,500 later, the first of three gum grafts was complete. Two more and my sinking teeth just might be back to sea level.

# 6

## SCRATCHING THE SURFACE

I cashed in on my Groupon for professional match-making services, looking forward to seeing what the company could do. They got to work right away and paired me up with an age-appropriate guy named Ryan. I had seen one very small photo of him, making our date not so much blind as slightly visually impaired.

We'd also spoken twice on the phone. Ryan called me for the first time on a Sunday, wanting to set up a date for Wednesday. He called again on Tuesday to cancel the Wednesday date—he was under the weather, and I didn't mind since I'd just had my gums grafted—and plan a new one for the following Sunday. During the brief rescheduling call we chatted about our plans for the weekend. That snippet of conversation gave me moderate to high expectations for the date, as did the improvement in my gums. I had upgraded my condition from "Franken-gums" to "Gum-zilla." I knew better than to flash a full-wattage smile, but a hearty grin seemed low-risk.

When I got to the restaurant, Ryan was at the bar, which is always a very promising start in my book. He bore a strong resemblance to the person in the photo the company had sent me, another step in the right direction. And when he stood up, he was a little taller than I am. I don't care much about height, but many men do, so I took that as a third good sign. I felt an initial attraction to him even if it was merely a superficial one.

Though I hadn't gone on a proper date in quite some time, I didn't feel nervous, nor did I stress over what we might talk about. (After the gum graft, I was more worried about mechanics than topics.) Our short exchanges on the phone had given me plenty of subjects to explore with Ryan, so the conversation never lagged. We also never wanted for subtext, which is crucial. Single people the world over understand that beneath the date that's visible to the public lies the date as experienced in the minds of the daters. The latter is the more important and almost always determines whether there's a next date. Here's an excerpt from our outing on Sunday.

**Me:** "During our phone chat, you said you were going to a wine tasting. How was it?"

**Subtext:** I like wine, in a non-twelve-step kind of way.

**Him:** "I really liked the first three vineyards we went to. The fourth and fifth weren't memorable."

**Subtext:** After the third place, you could've dragged my tongue across tree bark and I'd have enjoyed the finish.

**Me:** "Where did you go?"

**Subtext:** I got married at a vineyard. If it happens to be one of the places you toured, I will fake a salmonella outbreak.

**Me:** "So do you travel much for your job?"

**Subtext:** I can't miss you if you won't go away.

**Him:** "Hardly ever, though I do have a trip to Cincinnati this week."

**Subtext:** Unless you've always wanted to check out the World's Largest Ball of Twine in

Cawker City, Kansas, don't count on me for a boondoggle.

The dates both above and below the surface had gone quite well, and we both agreed that we should do it again.

Plans for the second outing took shape quickly. He suggested dinner and a movie at the mall. As date geometry goes, it was a square, but that was fine by me. The movie theater and the mall are two places I don't frequent, plus I had really wanted to see *Argo*. The movie let out just after 9 p.m., and Ryan suggested we grab a drink. This required me to relax my very firm policy against drinking at mall bars, but I agreed, because relationships are all about compromise. As Ryan sipped merlot and I sampled a mojito, our conversation meandered. Eventually it turned to Thanksgiving and families.

"I wish I had one," Ryan said, steering us straight toward a huge ditch I was sure he should've seen. When I filled out the form the service provided, I made clear that my biological clock had never ticked, and I wasn't about to wind it up now. I allowed for the possibility that I'd misunderstood his comment. During the first date he'd said something about his family living halfway across the country. Maybe he was referring to them instead of his hypothetical children.

To test my theory, I said, "You must miss your family, especially at the holidays. Do you wish they lived closer?" The look on his face told me I hadn't misunderstood. We'd landed in the ditch all right, and all four tires had gone flat.

Disagreement on whether to have kids is a known deal breaker. For the life of me I couldn't understand how a company that offers personalized matchmaking services could whiff on something so important. It's like going car shopping and telling the salesperson you've got your heart set on a manual transmission, only to have him show you a lot full of automatics. While perfectly fine, they give you a totally different driving experience than the one you had in mind, and I had no desire whatsoever to drive an automatic to Kid-ville.

As my mind began to compose a scathing letter to the service, I asked, "So, um, what are we doing here then?" (When I later described this moment to my friend Joseph, he said, "Wow. Totally awkward. I guess you can't ignore the elephant in the room when it craps on the rug." Joseph always says just the right thing.)

"I don't know." Ryan looked down, as if studying the merlot. "But I guess now's not the time to tell you the service says you're thirty-five." He snickered, but I could tell he wasn't joking.

His comment caused me to rethink my letter. I hadn't gotten deficient service. If anything, I got more than I paid for. Not only had the company identified a completely unsuitable suitor, they'd done all the lying for me. If that's not outstanding customer service in dating, I don't know what is.

# 7

## SISTER ACT

Instead of giving each other birthday presents this year, my sister Lynne and I decided to take a trip together. She had always wanted to go to South Beach in Miami, perhaps because it seemed like a true escape from her suburban, working mom existence. I hadn't spent much time there, so I thought it was a good choice, too. The plans came together quickly and we found ourselves there for a long weekend in mid-October. I'm pleased to report that our maiden joint voyage was a great trip overall; however, it was not entirely without incident.

I made a huge mistake early on by taking Lynne up on her offer to write a guest post for my blog without first asking what topic she had in mind. She wrote a detailed expose of my hotel room habits, stopping short of calling me "Pigpen," but otherwise showing no editorial restraint whatsoever.

My second major lapse in judgment occurred less than twelve hours after the first, when Lynne asked if I'd like to do a Jet Ski tour of Miami. I said yes, once again falling prey to the "why not?" philosophy that has tried to kill me several times over the course of my life. In my defense, Jet Skiing sounded like the perfect way to see the Miami skyline, check out major landmarks, and enjoy the water all at once.

On the morning of our tour, we took a thirty-minute cab ride from our hotel to the pickup spot at a marina on Biscayne Bay. The Jet Ski people had arranged our transport, which we later learned was not a real cab but an under-the-table hookup between the tour company and the off-duty cop who served as the marina "dockmaster" on the weekends. For a few extra bucks he was willing to leave the dock un-mastered so he could pick up a fare. Perhaps we should've taken that as a sign. On arriving at the marina, we signed a bunch of forms that made us responsible for anything bad that might happen during our outing, up to and including global warming. A guide then conducted a safety session that really put the "brief" in briefing.

"It's a little choppier than normal out there, so if it gets rough, try to remember to hit the gas," the guide said. "As weird as it sounds, the Jet Ski takes waves best at higher speeds." That was the extent of his advice.

Lynne and I excelled in the no-wake zone. After that, though, all bets were off. And so were my sunglasses, which the four-foot, white-capped swells claimed moments after I hit one of them head-on at a high rate of speed, just as I'd been instructed to do. The next wave that swamped me blasted off the thick coating of waterproof sunscreen I'd applied, along with the top layer of my skin.

The choppy seas affected the "tour" aspect of our trip too. At the halfway point our guide gave us a sign to pause. He came up to each person individually, an approach necessitated by the fact that we were bobbing up and down erratically, as if on aquatic pogo sticks. When he got to me, he gestured toward the series of tall buildings strung together along the shoreline. I waited, expecting the kind of locals-only insight you pay top dollar to get.

"That's the Miami skyline," he said. Satisfied that he'd given me my money's worth, he told me to turn around and get ready to head back.

On the return trip we rode with the current. While an improvement in some ways, catching large swells from behind doesn't cause the rider to spend any less time airborne. Lynne and I looked like Tom and Jerry on the high seas. We got back to the dock and sized each other up. My sister was covered in more salt than Lot's wife.

When we went inside the boathouse to retrieve our deposit, a staff member handed it to us and said, "Remember, our guide works for tips."

"Here's one," I said. "Don't take people out in these conditions."

The company offered no apology for the poor judgment it showed in sending us out (though they did cancel tours for the rest of the day) or for failing to live up to their advertising. In sum, we got more than we bargained for but less than we paid for.

I made the third big mistake of the trip when I opted to check my bag for the return flight. Little did I know that MIA would prove to be not just the three-letter code for Miami's airport, but also an acronym for the status of my luggage. It was nowhere to be found on the carousel at Dulles. My bag had last been spotted at the American Airlines curbside check-in in Miami, where the attendant took my rolling duffel and my sister's suitcase and put them on a cart behind him. Only one of the bags made it to Dulles alive.

Lynne and I headed straight for the customer service office, where the American Airlines agent told us my duffel didn't get on the flight. She made my bag sound lazy, as if it had been off smoking a pack of Camels when it should've been listening for the final boarding call. She took down my information and told me the bag should arrive at my house the next day.

I thanked her and added, "I trust you'll refund the checked bag fee," a statement so obvious I frankly thought that it went without saying. She shook her head, answering my non-question in the negative. I almost suggested that she apply for a customer service job with the Jet Ski people.

My lost luggage reminded me of another otherwise outstanding trip that had ended not with a bang but a splat. In 2002, just before I graduated law school, my friend Joseph and I decided we had to do something to celebrate my Last Spring Break Ever. Because law school tuition had depleted my savings, we snapped up a last-minute bargain with an affordable cruise line.

"A floating Walmart," Joseph later called it.

The travel gods rewarded me and Joseph handsomely for our procrastination. They sat us in first class on the flight from Washington to Fort Lauderdale. And instead of shoving us into the "closet-plus-porthole" category cabin we'd booked, they upgraded us to a stateroom. It had a sitting area, bar, balcony, and patio furniture. We didn't understand our good fortune, but we reveled in it and sailed in style to Grand Cayman, Cozumel, and New Orleans. Our extraordinary luck came to a screeching halt the final morning of the trip. I was packing my bags while Joseph did the customary sweep for forgotten items.

As he was pulling aside the curtains covering the sliding glass door that led to the balcony, I said, "I don't think you need to bother with that. I'm pretty sure I didn't leave anything out there."

He glanced outside and said, "You're right, there's nothing out there. And when I say 'nothing,' I really mean it." That didn't make any sense. "The furniture jumped ship," he said.

I went over to take inventory of the balcony for myself, and sure enough, it stood at zero items. Joseph and I couldn't think of anything to do besides wait for the cruise line to bill us. With heavy footsteps we walked the plank to shore and then made our way to the airport. The gods did not give us a smooth, first-class ride home. Instead, they put us in the back of the plane and shook it.

"I feel like a frog in a blender," Joseph muttered, head in hand. "Perfect way to end this cruise."

The guy sitting next to him must have heard this, because he said, "Oh, you were on the cruise too?" My ears pricked up and Joseph nodded. Apparently the guy and a few friends—all police officers in Rhode Island—had decided to take a vacation together and had booked the budget-friendly trip on a whim. Joseph asked him what he thought of the experience. Our new cop friend laughed.

"Well, it was great, but I felt sorry for the people staying next to us. I think it was a couple on their honeymoon and, well, we got a little rowdy toward the end."

"Oh, I wouldn't worry," Joseph said. "If they're typical newlyweds, they didn't even notice the noise."

The policeman chuckled. "Maybe not, but I bet they noticed their deck furniture was missing this morning." Joseph and I looked at each other, brows knitting. The cop paid no attention to our faces and kept right on talking, belly-laughing as he gave an un-coerced confession. "We...ha-ha-ha...threw...ha-ha-ha...it...ha-ha-ha...overboard!" Tears began to trickle down his cheeks.

Joseph's reaction mirrored my thoughts. "Great," he said. "I can hardly wait to tell the cruise people that four of Rhode Island's finest got drunk and decided to clean house."

I thought about that cruise experience as I took in the news about my MIA luggage and quickly realized losing one suitcase was nothing compared to misplacing an entire balcony full of rented furniture.

# 8

## RIGHT DOWN THE TUBES

**WARNING**: Several kindhearted men in my life have helped me with home repair on occasion. Those men—and you know who you are—should not read this.

My house escaped Hurricane Sandy unscathed, but a few days later the plumbing showed some signs of post-traumatic stress. The faucet choked and spluttered before exhaling a steady stream of water that took longer than usual to drain. The toilet wasn't itself either. Instead of performing the remove-and-replenish cycle smoothly, it took in a great gulp of air and then sent a little burst of water skyward, reminding me more of a surfacing whale than a working commode. I gave in to the stupid temptation that makes people try something again even when they're pretty sure they already know the outcome. Another mini-geyser. The toilet seemed exhausted afterward this time, because it didn't even bother to fill up the bowl all the way. Less than halfway through its job it gurgled ominously and then lapsed into silence.

When the plumbing started acting weird, I reached for the Google right away. A few weeks earlier I'd used the search engine to get my furnace working again. I had typed in a string of furnace-related terms and found a manual for my thermostat. The troubleshooting section suggested replacing the batteries. Aha! I hadn't even known the thing took batteries, never mind that the display had been flashing an icon that, in hindsight, did resemble a Duracell in distress. The fix itself was simple (unlike the process of prying the thermostat off the wall), and that little victory convinced me to make a permanent space in my toolbox for the Google.

A search of the toilet's symptoms turned up dozens of posts, all pointing in the same direction: blocked exterior vent. This theory had some intuitive appeal. The hurricane had strewn assorted debris all over the yard, so it wasn't much of a stretch to envision a stray squirrel getting plopped into the roof vent. I considered going up to the roof to check it out myself and learned that the Internet DIY community had opinions about that too. They thought it was a great idea if your main goal was to find an efficient way to wind up in traction.

I gave up on the idea of climbing the roof, but I didn't want to give up on fixing the problem myself until I knew I had tried everything I could. I approached the commode and, as required by my DNA, jiggled the handle. Handle-jiggling is my father's primary—no, only—solution to all plumbing maladies. No dice. Then I took the lid off and messed around with the arm-and-chain flushing mechanism. That wasn't the culprit either. Satisfied that I had done all I could, I gave up and called a plumber.

A two-man team arrived. I described the symptoms and led the men to the second-story bath. As I prepared to give them a demo, I worried that the toilet, after days of misbehaving, would suddenly act like a model loo. My fears were unfounded, thank goodness. The commode did exactly what I said it would, and I almost felt proud of it for not making me look like some ditzy chick who didn't know what she was talking about.

With great confidence I gave the plumbers my Google-based diagnosis. The larger guy looked dubious and said, "Ma'am, a blocked vent would be surprising unless everything else is backing up." I nodded knowingly. Google had told me the same thing, so

I pointed out that the sink had been draining very slowly.

The shorter plumber took the lid off the back of the toilet, flushed it, and watched its innards at work. Then he reached in, did something I couldn't see, and said, "You're all set."

What? He hadn't needed the ladder, or even applied so much as a dab of elbow grease. I requested a tutorial, and he happily obliged. It was the bowl refill tube, he explained. In all my Googling I had somehow failed to look closely at how this tube—the conduit that directs water back into the bowl post-flush—was connected and aimed. Or connected but misaimed in this case. All it needed was a little redirection. I made a lame attempt to save face.

"But what about the sink?" The plumbers indulged me again and pulled up the drain piece, bringing with it a large glob of black sludge. No tutorial was required to explain why the water took its time exiting the basin. I wouldn't want to go down there either.

For my airhead finale, I performed the Disappearing Checkbook Routine. My wallet had only $25 in cash and the plumbers didn't take credit cards. Online banking came to my rescue and enabled me to make the $125 payment for Commodes 101 electronically.

I started beating myself up for being unable to solve such a simple problem and for acting like a damsel in distress instead of a smart, independent woman. Then I got an idea.

"You know," I said to the plumbers as I walked them to the door, "you guys oughtta do a plumbing basics class for women. You'd make a fortune."

The first guy nodded, but the second didn't look like he was on board. "You can probably do it online already, ma'am," he said. "Just try Google."

# 9

## SOARING WITH THE TURKEYS

In November of 2011, I was in the middle of divorce proceedings and trying to unload the gigantic home my soon-to-be-ex and I had built on the lot where my old house once stood. My not-yet-former-husband refused to engage a Realtor and insisted that we sell the house, which I nicknamed the Yuppie Prison, on our own.

Since we both owned the house, I was forced to go along with his plan. The whole experience reminded me of Halloween 1979, when my best friend, Liz, and I hatched the brilliant idea to dress up as a two-headed man. This entailed squeezing ourselves into my father's old army jacket and poking my right arm and her left arm through the respective sleeves. Then we bound her right leg to my left. I don't know why we thought a two-headed man could only have three legs, but we did. As we limped along on three legs, tripping into the occasional living room as we went, it took us twice as long to get half the usual candy haul. We learned a powerful lesson that night: putting two heads together doesn't necessarily guarantee a better outcome.

I felt like an eight-year-old all over again as I found myself involuntarily joined at the hip with the man I was divorcing, like one-half of a two-headed real estate agent. Liz and I had at least agreed on where we wanted to go and how to get there, whereas my soon-to-be-ex and I lacked any kind of shared vision or direction. Our partnership, if you could even call it that, functioned less like Fred Astaire and Ginger Rogers than Bugs Bunny and Elmer Fudd.

We got an offer on the Yuppie Prison just before Halloween. The typically routine process of contract ratification became a time-crunched ordeal, complete with the two-headed real estate monster scrambling at 11:30 p.m. to find a working fax machine and make a transmittal by midnight. The closing date was set for the end of November, with a final inspection scheduled for the weekend of Thanksgiving. This cast a pall over my holiday, in part because it forced me to cancel a trip I'd planned with my friend Joseph.

On Thanksgiving night, Joseph and I were supposed to board a plane for London. There, we would meet up with a group of his British friends who celebrate our American holiday in their own special way. The event is shrouded in secrecy (and a haze of red wine), so I can't divulge details, but I can disclose some figures that might help you picture it. By my calculations the festivities are 5 percent sacred, 30 percent profane, and 65 percent Monty Python. I had been so excited about that London trip that year, only to find myself having far too much in common with the Thanksgiving turkey: both of us desperately needed to escape, and neither of us could fly.

My friends in the UK felt my pain. They sent me a message of encouragement that still brings me comfort, along with a few other choice emotions. I replicate it here in its entirety, save a few revisions that were necessary to preserve a shred of decency.

> *Oh, that is sad! We are all glum. We were SO looking forward to seeing you again. Karen, I want you to radiate love, compassion, and forgiveness throughout the house sale process. Emanating positive energy will ensure that both of you let go in a healthy karma-minimizing way...then as you walk away from those signed documents may this*

*message from the London herd ring in your ears: [Vulgar verb] him and the vehicle that he drove in on. The commonly held wisdom during break-ups is that your friends should remain neutral. Well, we blow that out of the group orifice. You rock and don't let anyone tell you otherwise—EVER. Granted the collective who are shouting this out are questionable, but better to hear our voices than dwell on the deeds and words of a [vulgar adjective + vulgar noun] who has committed the worst relationship crime ever: not embracing and therefore plain long-term adoring your particular brand of greatness. Can I elicit a group London "Amen" now please?*

This year I'll be in the first wave of pilgrims at Heathrow, and I can hardly wait.

# 10

## SWEATING THE SMALL STUFF

For some families, the process of getting a Christmas tree consists of driving a few miles and braving the wilds of the Home Depot parking lot. For my tribe, it's an expedition. We trek to the Virginia countryside and spend hours wandering its rolling hills, combing acres of spruces, firs, and pines in search of perfect specimens. We Yankoskys apply more care and scrutiny to the process of cutting down a Christmas tree than preparing our tax returns.

In 2011, I didn't pick out a tree of my own because I was living with my sister and her family as I slogged through my divorce. Once I bought a house, I was again excited about the hunt and couldn't wait to start decorating my own tree. My collection of ornaments had lived in a box for two years, seeing daylight only briefly when it became an unexpected source of controversy while I was dissolving my marriage.

When the decision to divorce isn't made jointly, arguments can arise about anything, including the rights to specific oxygen molecules. But since my future-ex-husband and I had a very large fish to fry— unloading the enormous house we'd built, through the For Sale By Owner process no less—I was surprised to find myself caught up in a melee over holiday tchotchkes one Saturday in November of 2011.

I'd spent the day at the Yuppie Prison, obtaining estimates from contractors on the few items the prospective buyers required us to fix before closing. As one of those contractors explained his plans to bridge a gap in the seal between the custom-built front doors, I phoned my co-owner so he could hear the contractor's plan and consent to having the work done. When he didn't answer, I left a message.

Seconds after I left the voice mail, he emailed me. The message didn't relate to the door, or the pile of paperwork I'd put together to sell the house, or my request that we meet to review the documents together, given our lack of real estate expertise. His e-mail was about… Christmas ornaments. He asserted that I'd intentionally taken them when I moved out. He wanted to meet with me all right, but not to discuss the house. He wanted to claim his share of the holiday decorations.

A person of average intellect would grasp the significance of the Christmas ornaments and agree that they warranted a separate, focused meeting, whereas something less important, like the imminent sale of our home, did not; however, since my intellect was subpar, something my not-yet-ex-husband had pointed out several times over the course of the divorce, I was able to vault right past his common sense approach and suggest that we meet first about the house. After several rounds of discussion, he gave in, perhaps because he recognized that sometimes you have to compromise on minor stuff before you can get to the big-ticket items. (I later told a friend the whole conversation was so bizarre and illogical that I might as well have been trying to reason with a lawnmower. That comment led us to start referring to my once-husband as the Lawnmower, or the LM for short.)

That the man even thought about Christmas ornaments, much less cared about them, surprised me. Time and again during our separation, the LM told me he wanted no reminders of me. On top of that, he hadn't even owned any holiday trinkets before we met in 2009 because he hadn't bothered with a tree during his single days. The baubles that adorned our joint trees were pretty much all mine. Friends and family had given them to me, with a very large influx in 2003 courtesy of an intervention two of my friends staged when they laid eyes on my first tree.

"Oh, honey, that is the saddest thing we've ever seen," they had said, sizing up my tree and finding its unintentionally minimalist style deficient. They couldn't bear to let me persist in a state of decorative famine, and they continue to give me two ornaments every year just to make sure my inventory never again drops to dangerously low levels.

It was true that during our time together, the LM and I had picked up some solid-colored balls and a dozen or so other ornaments at after-Christmas sales, along with a tree-topping angel. I had thought that stuff was living somewhere at his house, but unbeknownst to me I had somehow ended up with our tiny stash of joint decorative property. The items were packed in a large plastic bin that I hadn't opened since moving.

I had no sentimental attachment to the jointly acquired ornaments. Most of them were not exactly my taste, by which I mean I'd have thought twice before donating them to a foundation for the blind. The angel, in particular, had a face that could've ruled the nightmare kingdom every bit as effectively as the clown from *Poltergeist*.

I had no qualms about giving up that stuff and did so immediately. The LM wasn't satisfied, continuing to accuse me of petty larceny, but eventually he agreed to drop the issue. In hindsight, I could have resolved the whole debate a lot earlier by just giving him all the Christmas stuff, no matter its origins. Had I been thinking clearly at the time, I would have recognized that the value of the trinkets stemmed from my relationship with the people who gave them to me. Those relationships were stronger than ever, so I wouldn't have lost a thing if I had walked away without so much as a single gold ball.

Still, I'm not entirely sorry that I stood my ground. I'm excited about opening the bin this year and can hardly wait to see my little buddies and hang them up, no strings attached.

# 11

## UNSAFE AT ANY SPEED

I view dating as just another adventure. So does a good friend of mine who, like me, is a lawyer and also recently divorced. I'll call her "Amber," because she requested it, and it's the least I can do for someone who agreed to let me write about her love life. Since we're so similarly situated, Amber and I decided to embark on a joint adventure: speed dating. At most speed dating events, participants talk one-on-one for a few minutes before moving on to another victim. Amber managed to find one of these round robins with a unique theme: the Myers-Briggs personality indicator.

The MB indicator, according to the official website, classifies personality based on a person's preferences about perception and judgment in the following areas:

**Favorite world:** Do you prefer to focus on the outer world or on your own inner world? This is called Extraversion (E) or Introversion (I).

**Information:** Do you prefer to focus on the basic information you take in or do you prefer to interpret and add meaning? This is called Sensing (S) or Intuition (N).

**Decisions:** When making decisions, do you prefer to first look at logic and consistency or first look at the people and special circumstances? This is called Thinking (T) or Feeling (F).

**Structure:** In dealing with the outside world, do you prefer to get things decided or do you prefer to stay open to new information and options? This is called Judging (J) or Perceiving (P).

Once you answer a bunch of questions that help you specify your preference in each category, you end up with a composite that reflects your personality type, expressed as a four-letter code. Speaking in code is a real boon for people with my personality type, because "INFP" sounds way better than "flaky, emotional shut-in." A Myers-Briggs-oriented event sounded like it would be right up my alley. Amber and I registered. The event took place on Sunday evening, a few hours after I'd gone with my family on our annual expedition to find Christmas trees. Amber and I decided to meet at the restaurant early for a pregame cocktail.

"So first you hunted Christmas trees and now men, eh?" she said as she took the stool next to mine. I could only hope the speed dating would go half as well as the tree hunt had.

I canvassed the restaurant. As of that moment, the herd looked quite thin. Six patrons sat at the bar, including us, and we looked like the only singletons. We chalked up the sparse pickings to our early arrival and chatted happily while sipping wine and waiting for kickoff. When the time came, we checked in. The organizers handed us name tags that reflected our four-letter personality profile and also indicated which MB types would match best with us. They claimed that INFPs get along with just about anyone, which explained how I'd managed to cover the full personality spectrum in making disastrous mate selections. Amber and I headed to our seats. It still didn't look like either side had enough players to field a full team, but the men were really hurting. In hindsight, I wish they'd forfeited.

The first guy I met, Tom, said he'd gone speed dating several times and had really enjoyed it. This statement led me to believe he had some experience making conversation. And yet, when I handed the conversational football off to him, he didn't even attempt to grab it. Instead, he was off in some remote corner of the field, picking daisies. I had to recover my own fumble. After four minutes I was thrilled to drop back and punt. Chris was the next guy in my rotation. He looked like a grown-up version of Long Duk Dong from *Sixteen Candles* and had the dating skills to match. Somehow the topic of age came up. I couldn't have guessed his –I can't guess anyone's – and said as much. He cocked his head to the side and studied my face.

"You're probably ten years older than me," he said, radiating confidence.

"Well, how old are you?"

"Thirty-five," he said.

"I'm forty-one," I said. Apparently the four minutes I spent with him didn't just feel like four years, they looked like four years.

The rounds I enjoyed most that night were the ones I spent without a partner, reading e-mail on my phone while I sat on the proverbial bench. I guess Myers-Briggs got it right: I really do prefer to focus on my own inner world.

# 12

## JUST PUT THAT ANYWHERE

My family has its share of proud Christmas traditions. Somewhere along the way, we moved them over to make room for a slightly less proud one: gag gifts. I can't pinpoint the year when prank presents nudged their way onto our Christmas scene, but I think it started with me and my brother in the early 1990s. Now all nine Yank adults—and often several extended Yanks—play along, and we live for it. Don't get me wrong: we adults love watching the kids unwrap presents from Santa. But we're every bit as excited to get to punch lines that have been twelve months or longer in the making, and we're usually rewarded for our wait. A few years ago, for example, my sister Lynne was given a giant mass of panties bound together by rubber bands because she tends to get her undies in a wad.

For the last two years, someone has gotten a mailbox. (Every family has its natural enemies, and ours are postal receptacles.) Lynne's husband, Paul, was the first mailbox recipient, thanks to an incident that happened in the summer of 2010 as he and Lynne were wrapping up a visit with our sister Suzi and her family. As my brother-in-law backed out of the driveway, he crashed into Suzi's mailbox, wiping it out.

The mailbox had my name on it last year. I got it because of a couple of episodes involving the letter catcher at the Yuppie Prison the Lawnmower and I built and then sold (on our own, while divorcing) that November, without ever having occupied it. During the construction process, we had disagreed about where the mailbox should go. This disheartened but didn't surprise me because we'd found it challenging to agree on most house-related issues. Ultimately I disengaged and let my then-husband select both the box and its location. He had it placed at the foot of the driveway, which I pointed out seemed dangerously close to the driveway itself.

I proved myself right in a most unsatisfying fashion one Saturday morning when, after an argument had made me late for my niece's swim meet, I attempted a hasty exit and decapitated the mailbox with the back of my car. Shortly thereafter my husband declared the box irreparable and presented me with a bill for it.

Since we were still together at the time, this came as a bit of a shock. I thought marriage meant exchanging vows, not invoices. Even more shocking was the $600 price tag. If I had $600 to burn, I'd put it toward a flight to Rome, or at the very least dental work, rather than a fancy home for pizza coupons. I promised to replace it pronto with something that would serve the same purpose, even if it didn't look exactly the same as the original.

"Function over form," I'd said.

Apparently the prospect of me exercising unfettered discretion in mailbox selection spurred him to find a way to salvage the old one, and the problem was solved. It was one of our better compromises. Soon that minor triumph was eclipsed by more divisive events, like our separation and decision to put the house on the market. In November of 2011, a few months after we listed the Yuppie Prison, I received a call from a real estate agent who had just shown it to a couple of prospective inmates.

"They're very interested in the property. That's the good news," she said. It was spectacular news as far as I was concerned, because it was the first serious bite we'd gotten since we'd started advertising it in August.

"What's the bad news then?"

"Um, well, as the husband was backing out of the driveway, he slammed into the mailbox." She paused to let the news sink in. "He did some damage, I'm afraid." It was the best bad news I'd ever heard, so much so that it inspired me to make a special trip to the house to check out the crime scene. At the foot of the driveway stood the post, in pristine condition. The mailbox itself sat in the grass, leaned up against the post as if waiting for the next bus. Those homebuyers had delivered, all right.

And so did Paul, who drew my name for the annual gag gift exchange last year and bequeathed the mailbox to me (along with a T-shirt featuring Charlie Sheen and the caption "WINNING!").

Gag gift season is upon us again, and I think the mailbox is ready for a change of address.

# 13

## A LITTLE OFF-KEY

"Hope you're around for the obligatory Christmas visit," Dave and Donna had written in their annual card, which arrived late last week. They're close friends from my law school days, and I see them regularly, including during the holidays. They always encourage me to bring a guest when I come over, but I'll be going solo this year, and not just because I'm in between significant others. I love my pals, but on the rare occasions when I've brought a date to their house, things haven't gone too well.

There was the time, back in 2007, when they invited me and my then-boyfriend, John, to their house for a dinner party. An assistant dean from the law school and her husband rounded out the guest list. The dean had introduced me to Dave when he and I were first-year law students at George Mason University in the fall of 1998, and she took a personal interest in both of us that she maintained even after we graduated. She always kept an eye out for dating prospects for me, so I was excited to introduce her to John.

I knew she'd like the fact that he was un-lawyerly, kind, and tall. She'd also appreciate his success as an entrepreneur, whether or not she was a fan of the on-line gaming industry he worked in. I suspected she'd view his laid-back, reserved nature a good complement to my chattiness. And she might have, except it didn't look so complementary when John withered in the face of her steady stream of questions. John looked relieved when she shifted the focus away from him. Eventually his look of relief gave way to a face of boredom. He tried to hide it, but the occasional flare of his nostrils as he nose-yawned revealed his true feelings.

We moved into the dining room. John was moderately engaged but seemed uncomfortable, perhaps because his taste in chair styles leaned more toward beanbag than Queen Anne. As we dined on pork loin, he followed the conversation, in the sense that he was always a step or two behind it. The evening was not unfolding as I had envisioned. After dinner, I could tell John was ready to go. Just as I was about to start the good-bye process, Donna asked me to play their piano. She and Dave made this request any time I visited. Though I don't like to play for other people, I usually obliged them, but this time I really didn't want to prolong my departure.

I said, "Oh, you all have better things to do than sit around and listen to me bang on a piano." The dean dismissed my objection with a wave of her hand.

"You have to indulge us at least a little bit before you go. I've never heard you play." She said this as if all those years she'd been missing out on Sergei Rachmaninov instead of an amateur who'd taken lessons as a kid and still remembered how to play a few tunes. With great reluctance, I followed the group into the living room. I hoped John might at least welcome the change of venue and a respite from lawyer talk. After I played a jazz number and a ballad, the dean asked me to play a classical piece. I knew just the thing: a rollicking, challenging Beethoven allegro. I had just gotten through the toughest part, a set of fast-paced arpeggios at opposite ends of the keyboard, and was nearing the end of the piece. I caught a glimpse of the dean's face. She wore a tiny frown that I took as a sign of interest.

I glanced at Dave and Donna. They looked engaged. I stole a peek at John. He looked...asleep. The dean may well have been interested in my piece, but she was plainly transfixed by the sight of my boyfriend on the loveseat, eyes closed, head back, and mouth ajar. The sound of hands clapping woke him up, but I barely heard it over the voice of the fat lady warming up in the wings.

My next boyfriend, Steve, came to dinner at Donna and Dave's too. Steve was eleven years my junior and had a huge, fun personality to match his king-size smarts. That night, a few nonacademic guests attended in place of the dean and her husband, and there was no playing of the piano. (Perhaps my friends feared touching off another relationship-ending bout of narcolepsy.)

But some playing did occur. At some point after dinner, Steve ended up in the basement rec room, horsing around with Dave and Donna's teenaged son and his friends. I can't blame Steve for choosing the kids over us. They were, after all, closer to his age. But I did blame him for causing a collision that left a large hole in the drywall, bringing yet another swift and awkward close to an evening at Dave and Donna's.

Yep, "plus none" is definitely the way to go this year.

# 14

## THIS ROUND'S ON ME

My parents moved to the Washington, D.C. area in 1972, so I had assumed they'd visited most of the local institutions multiple times. Just before Christmas last year I learned that they had missed one: the Round Robin Bar at the Willard InterContinental Hotel downtown. My sister Lynne and I decided to remedy that in short order by inviting them to join us there for a cocktail on December 26.

The Willard sits mere steps from the White House and, according to its website, is known as the "Crown Jewel of Pennsylvania Avenue." Aside from its elegant architecture, the hotel's site recounts quite an impressive history as well:

A most celebrated historic Washington DC hotel, the Willard InterContinental Washington, has been the focal point for elegant dinners, meetings, and gala social events for more than 150 years. An institution, this grand Washington DC historic hotel has hosted almost every US president since Franklin Pierce in 1853. On August 28, 1963, the Reverend Martin Luther King finished his famous "I Have A Dream" speech while a guest at the Willard. Other notable guests have included Charles Dickens, Buffalo Bill, David Lloyd George, P. T. Barnum, Lord and Lady Napper, and countless others. Walt Whitman mentioned the hotel in his works; and Mark Twain penned two books here in the early 1900s. Throughout the ages, no phrase has raised eyebrows like "I'm staying at the Willard."

The last sentence really nails it. If any member of the Yank tribe mentioned in casual conversation that we were staying at the Willard, it would raise eyebrows at the very least. It's no secret that we are not, how shall I say, Willard people. But I figured we could fake it long enough to get through a round of drinks.

Lynne and I met our parents in the lobby, and the four of us made our way to the fabled lounge, a smallish room with curved green walls, a clubby old-school feel, and a round bar at the center. It's the perfect geometric complement to the Oval Office a few doors down. We settled into one of the black leather booths that rim the room and took in our surroundings.

"Can you imagine the wheeling and dealing that's gone on in here?" Mom said as she glanced around. We soon turned our attention to the drink menu. The stratospheric prices didn't surprise me, but they caught my father off guard.

"I've never paid seven dollars for a Budweiser," Dad said, raising one eyebrow and fixing me with a look my siblings and I know well. It always conveys the same unspoken message: "You kids don't appreciate the value of money."

I flashed him the smile of a Willard person, which said, "Eighteen dollars for a drink is nothing. I've paid more for six ounces of non-organic tap water." When the waiter arrived moments later, I proceeded to order one of the most expensive mixed drinks on the menu. Lynne and Mom followed suit immediately, causing Dad to admit defeat and order a marked-up Bud.

When the waiter came back with our drinks, he dropped off a cone of potato chips to help keep our thirst whetted. The chips didn't tempt me much. They looked like standard fare, plus my teeth prefer sweet over savory every time. My father, on the other hand, loves salty snacks and reached right in. We could tell from his expression that these chips had spoken to him in a way that garden-variety Lay's never had.

"What do they put on these things? I keep eating 'em even though I already feel like a bloated toad," said Dad, possibly bringing a new expression to a place that thought it had heard everything.

When the waiter came back to our table, my sister asked, "What kind of chips are those? Our dad really liked them, in case you couldn't tell." She pointed to the now-empty cone.

He smiled and shrugged—Willard people probably don't inquire about potato chip heritage all that often—and said, "I don't know, but I'll find out."

"We'll have another round while you're at it," Dad said. Apparently the chips eliminated whatever hesitation he had about forking over seven more bucks for a mass-produced domestic beer. The waiter returned with a tray that held our drinks. As he set them down, he gave me a conspiratorial nod in the direction of his tray. I didn't understand at first, and then I noticed that his right hand held something else beneath the tray: a bag of Route 11 potato chips. He inched his hand ever so slightly my way so I could grab the bag on the sly. I immediately stuffed it into my purse, as any Willard person would do. The next time the waiter came by, we asked for the check.

"It would be my pleasure," he said with a gracious smile.

As he turned to walk away, I grabbed his elbow and whispered a request to bring the bill to me. Lynne and I wanted to treat our parents, a feat that's about as easy to pull off as levitation. We've succeeded at most a handful of times, and only then through the kind of covert operations that would qualify us for employment at the CIA. A few minutes later, I saw the waiter approaching out of the corner of my eye. While the rest of the table kept talking, I extended a hand behind me like a relay runner preparing for a baton exchange. The waiter slipped the check into my hand without a word. Our stealth hand-off had escaped my parents' attention, if not my sister's.

I held the folio under the table in one hand and pulled my purse onto my lap with the other so Dad wouldn't notice me reaching for my wallet. Though I couldn't see the contents of my wallet, I really didn't need to. The Visa I used for everything always occupied the first spot in the sleeve of credit cards. I slid out the top card, tucked it into the folio on my lap, and slipped it into the waiter's hand. To create an additional diversion, my sister asked our server to take a group photo, as you do when you're a Willard person. He smiled, obliged her, and then headed off in the direction of the bar.

As we waited for the server to come back with the rest of the paperwork, my father said, "Well, I thought you two had lost your minds, wanting to take us somewhere like this. But it's a pretty neat place, so I'd say this was one of your better ideas." Lynne and I beamed, because parental approval always feels good, no matter how old you are. Moments later the waiter returned. I was still smiling as he handed me the folio that held the bill.

"I'm sorry, ma'am," he said. "We can't accept payment with a Safeway card."

My parents' and sister's smiles turned into full-blown laughter.

"Let me get this straight," my father said, pausing to wipe tears from his eyes. "You tried to pay for drinks, at the *Willard,* with a *grocery* card?" That sent them all into another fit of ab-crunching laughter. While they cackled I produced a viable credit card and handed it to the waiter.

Once the transaction was complete, I rounded up my dignity and the Route 11 chips and left with my sister and parents in tow. We decided that very night to make the Round Robin trip a new holiday tradition. When we return to the scene of the crime this year, I'll have my Harris-Teeter card at the ready.

# 15

## A BIRD IN THE HAND
## IS WORTH...ZILCH

Yesterday I had lunch with my friend Greg. Once a mere law firm acquaintance, he became a friend in 2011 when he realized I needed a distraction from my divorce and invited me to join him and his buddies on a hike in the Blue Ridge Mountains.

Greg loves all kinds of outdoors activities, including hunting. But he's not one of those people who hunts just for sport; he's a conservationist. Whatever he shoots ends up on his dinner table. Over lunch he told me about a trip he'd taken to Idaho since last I'd seen him. He listed the names of the birds he'd hunted—which fed his family and their guests at Thanksgiving— and paused after he said "chukar." (As glamorous as this word looks, its unexotic pronunciation is: "chucker.")

"You probably haven't heard of those, have you, Karen?"

"Oh, I know what chukars are," I said, waving him on. He looked surprised, a perfectly understandable reaction since I learned everything I know about birds from a Fisher-Price Speak and Say.

"You do? Really? I've hardly met anyone who does. How in the world do you know about chukars?" I explained that my ex-husband had enjoyed hunting them too, something I discovered a few months before we got married.

My then-fiance had reached deep in the freezer one Saturday morning in search of something to defrost for dinner that night. He pulled out a couple masses of aluminum foil and said, "We'd better hurry up and eat these." The foil blobs had a roundish shape that revealed nothing about their contents. They could have been tofurkey balls for all I knew, and I didn't want to take any chances.

"What are they?" I asked.

"Chukars," he said. As you can imagine, his response did little to advance my comprehension. Based on the name alone I pictured tenders made of various bird parts all pressed together—the poultry equivalent of particle board—until he explained that a chukar is a species of bird that hails from the pheasant family. After checking it out on Wikipedia, I decided that it looks like a partridge that accessorizes with animal prints. Apparently my betrothed and a few of his buddies had shot several chukars on a hunting trip months before I arrived on the scene, so these birds were ripe for the eating. I watched with great curiosity as he unwrapped the foil. What he extracted from it was unremarkable.

"Looks like chicken," I said.

He nodded and said, "Tastes like chicken too." As we ate dinner that night, I decided he was right. It did taste like chicken, especially if you like your chicken sprinkled with birdshot. I enjoy a good food texture surprise as much as the next person, but not when it endangers my dental work.

After I told Greg the backstory on my introduction to chukars, he asked, "Where did your ex go to hunt them?"

"Somewhere near Lexington." One of the Lawnmower's friends had a house in the country relatively close to there. It served as a base when the group got together to hunt.

"Lexington? As in the town in Virginia?" Greg said. I nodded. "Impossible. Chukars aren't native to the East Coast. They like rocky, arid terrain and inhabit the western part of the United States. In fact, the chukar is the official bird of Pakistan." I felt like I was having lunch with Alex Trebek. I laughed, but Greg's face showed no trace of humor.

"Listen, Karen, I've really tried not to pass judgment on this guy because I haven't met him."

This was something I'd long admired about Greg. He rarely rushed to conclusions about people. As a litigator who had spent countless hours conducting depositions and preparing witnesses, Greg understood that stories are multifaceted creatures and that the truth can be elusive prey, especially when emotions are involved. Whenever I talked about the divorce, he would listen with empathy, like all of my friends. But unlike most of them, not to mention every single one of my family members, Greg refrained from maligning the LM, and I appreciated that. Blind loyalty has its place, but so does fairness, and I knew I hadn't behaved perfectly during my marriage. Greg put down the fork that held his next bite of carnitas and rice. His face, normally impassive, looked indignant and serious.

"The fact that he hunted had been a redeeming quality in my book, but now that I know he shoots preserve birds? That's not even real hunting. It's cheating!" he scoffed.

I wondered how long Greg had been waiting for me to hand him a piece of non-emotional information that would give him permission to fall off the fence of neutrality and onto my side. Without even meaning to, I'd done it. All it took was giving him the bird.

# 16

## THE UNEASY WAY OUT

Like many women, I dread going to the hair salon. I appreciate the results but detest spending hours in a chair with strips of aluminum foil poking out from my head as if trying to improve the reception in my brain. But for once, I was almost looking forward to my upcoming appointment. I had scheduled it for a Friday in late December, which proved fortuitous for two reasons. First, I had been asked out on a date for that very night, giving me a chance to present my coif in its most favorable light. Second, I had questions about my date's hair. I had reason to believe it might not be his own, and I hoped my stylist could help me figure out how to conduct a proper evaluation. In all my years of dating, I hadn't run across that issue before.

"What makes you think his hair isn't real?" Jessie asked with complete neutrality as she snipped. She's the best stylist I've ever had, not just because of her skill but because she's as honest as she is open-minded. Her tone implied no judgment whatsoever of fake-haired men or the women who date them.

"I'm not sure all of it's fake, Jessie. I think maybe just part of it is."

"Ah, so a toupee, then? You know, Karen, a lot of men your age—" I cut her off before she could complete the sentence, which could not possibly have ended well for me.

"That's just the thing. I don't think it's a toupee because, oddly enough, the top was the part that looked natural. It was salt and peppery, you know? And when he ran his fingers through it, the strands seemed to move one at a time, like real hair does."

"Okay, so if the top was real, then dot, dot, dot?" Jessie sometimes ends her sentences this way instead of framing an actual question, which is something you can pull off if you're hip and twenty-six, like she is.

"So what's the problem, right? The sides. That's what looked off. The texture, the color, I don't know. Something about them didn't seem...real." Jessie stopped cutting so her mirror image could look mine right in the eye.

"Hold on a minute. Are you saying he faked the sides?"

I nodded. Her look of unabashed horror told me that, though she'd seen plenty of hair crimes, this atrocity was beyond even her imagination. I guess Jessie wasn't as nonjudgmental as I'd thought. She regained her professional demeanor and decided that it could be hereditary. I was perfectly happy to accept that explanation because it gave me hope. To be clear, the particular hope I was nurturing was not that the guy had hair on his head—male baldness has never fazed me—but rather that whatever was going on up there was natural. (For some reason, I just can't abide hair fakeness in men. Yes, I know it's a double standard.) After tipping Jessie well for giving me great hair and some date optimism, I headed home.

A few hours later I was back in my car, driving to Bethesda to meet Sam for our date. He had asked to meet at six, which surprised me and called to mind visions of early bird specials and Jessie's unfortunate "men your age" lead-in. Maybe he just wanted to have drinks. As I entered the restaurant I spotted Sam at the bar. A big smile spread across his face as he hopped off the stool and walked toward me.

He gave me a warm hug, kissed me on the cheek, and said, "It's really great to see you again, Karen."

"You too," I said.

As we headed toward the host stand, Sam said he had been nervous about our date. I should have found his candid admission endearing, but it made me bristle instead. I can't explain exactly why. Maybe it shattered my illusion that a first date is no big deal, just two people socializing for an hour or two. Sam's open acknowledgement of nerves implied expectations. Suddenly, our first date, which moments ago had been roaming around without a care in the world, would feel like it had to measure up to something. Rare is the first date that performs well under that kind of pressure.

The maître d' offered us our choice of two tables. The first was nestled in a three-table alcove with a sign that read "Lover's Lane" over the entrance. The second sat right next to the drafty front door. These choices flat-out stunk. One location would require me to spend the evening warding off a chill, while the implications of the other might require me to promote one. Sam was ready to head to Lover's Lane but deferred the decision to me. With some reluctance, I agreed it was the better option for climate-based reasons.

The waiter arrived moments later and said, "Hi there. I'm Mike, and I'll be your server this evening."

"Nice to meet you, Mike. I'm Sam." I assumed Mike told us his name so we would know who to ask for if we needed something, not because he expected us to tell him ours in return or intended to establish a personal relationship. Sam then proceeded to say Mike's name with the frequency of a Publisher's Clearinghouse letter. It made me squirm.

Moments after handing us menus and a wine list, Mike asked if we needed the special Groupon menu. It offered appetizers, dinner, and dessert for $40. Sam said he didn't have a Groupon, but the lure of a three-course deal prompted him to fish out his phone and try to buy one on the fly. Never before had a first date gone on clearance right before my very eyes. After half a minute that felt like half an hour, Sam abandoned the Groupon quest. I was relieved because, at 6:00 p.m., I was barely ready for a snack, much less three courses. But I was more than ready for a drink, so I reached for the wine list.

"I love wine too," Sam said. "In fact, just last night I opened a 1995 Caymus Napa Cab Sav."

I knew Caymus because of my failed marriage to a lover of expensive wine. Sam's casual mention of a $150 bottle would have made his attempt to Groupon me all the more confounding had I not witnessed many such displays of selective frugality while I was married to the Lawnmower. The LM kept an expensive convertible in the driveway, two high-end Italian motorcycles in the garage, and a wine collection worth thousands of dollars, yet he bought generic tuna fish and soda. Justly or not, Sam's comment sent a red flag sailing up the pole.

"Maybe I could bring one of those bottles to share with you on our next date," he said, casting a hopeful look my way. I picked up my wine glass and took a big sip so I wouldn't have to say anything. I seemed to be the only one who saw that the chances of a second date were dimming.

Being in closer proximity to Sam and his hair dealt another blow to the second date's chances. Without even having to consider DNA, I could see that the issue I spotted when I first met Sam was not confined to the sides after all. It was more, how shall I say, systemic. I cannot criticize anyone for vanity—especially since I had spent $150 and two hours that same day to make my hair look its unnatural best—but I wish he and other similarly situated men would just embrace the baldness.

Though our conversation flowed quite naturally, unlike our respective hairdos, it lacked the witty banter that had first attracted me to Sam. Eventually I asked him how his Christmas had been. The topic had come up the evening we first met. He'd told me then that his pending divorce meant that he would be without his kids on Christmas for the first time. One doesn't have to be a parent to appreciate how wrenching that must be, so on Christmas Day itself I had sent him a text to wish him a good day despite the circumstances. He'd sent a "thanks" in response but that was it.

"It went better than I expected, even though I was alone," he said. "That text you sent meant a lot. It's pretty unusual for someone to be so thoughtful and caring."

"You're nice to say that, but I hope it's not unusual. I figure most people, especially us single types, think about things like that during the holidays."

"I don't think they do, Karen," he said. "Even if we never go out again, which I hope we do, I want you to know that I think you're great."

He had referred to a possible second date approximately 2,487 times over the course of the evening. Only our waiter's name got mentioned more often. The two even got mentioned in the same sentence when Sam said, "Mike, if she wants to see the dessert menu, does that mean she'll go out with me again?" Sam seemed intent on continuing the drive down Lover's Lane, but I had begun to look for an exit ramp. Picking up the tab is my standard way out of a date that's going poorly, and I intended to follow the route that I knew.

Mike reappeared with the bill in hand. I got ready to reach for it, fully prepared to dislocate my shoulder if necessary. Sadly, I never had a chance because he handed it directly to Sam. I reached into my purse, took out my wallet, and asked Sam if I could contribute. (After the Groupon thing I figured I had a decent shot.)

"No way, Karen. You can get it the next time. Or maybe I can cook for you, and we can have a really nice bottle of wine. And you could play the piano." The piano was a topic that had come up when we first met too. I'd told Sam that night, and reiterated as Mike took the check, that playing for others makes me self-conscious unless I know them quite well.

"Well, pretty soon you might know me *very* well," he said, waggling his eyebrows suggestively. That one tiny facial gesture annihilated any chances for a second date and guaranteed that we would never know each other on the level he was implying.

"Um, about that," I said as I fiddled with the cloth napkin in my lap. "I really appreciated dinner and enjoyed our conversation, but...I don't see us dating."

"Why not?" Sam said.

"Whoops, that's what I get for not thinking two conversational steps ahead. Heh-heh," I said, stalling. Sam didn't chuckle. He sat there, stone-faced and silent, waiting for me to continue. "It's hard to explain..." By this time, I had worked the napkin into a ball. "I just don't think we're...a fit."

"I agree completely," he said.

"Really?" A legitimate laugh escaped me before I could stop it. "Ha-ha, I'm glad to hear it!" I said. And if I'd stopped speaking right then and there, everything would've been great. Instead, "why?" managed to sneak right past security and out of my mouth. Sam answered as if he'd been waiting for that question all night.

"For starters, you're not my type at all, Karen. I mean you're attractive, but I couldn't imagine kissing you. And then there's this whole, I don't know, *affect* about you." He wrinkled his nose as if in response to a passing skunk. I was unable to stifle a snort. I found it funny that the same man who seemed eager to connect

Biblically only moments earlier now found me repulsive and was dismissing as fake the very thoughtfulness he'd just praised as unusual.

I attempted a gracious smile and said, "Well then, it all worked out perfectly, didn't it? Shall we?"

Sam stood up and exited Lover's Lane with the urgency of a police chase. He had reached the front door while I was still in the alcove, putting on my scarf and coat. I think he would have left me altogether but for the presence of the maître d', who knew we were on a date because Sam had announced it when I'd arrived. Sam and I soon discovered we had parked in the same garage across the street. His car was one space away from mine, which meant he couldn't avoid me altogether.

As he opened his car door he said, "Take care and happy New Year," without so much as looking at me. The absurdity of it all triggered yet another inappropriate laugh.

"I guess so, if that's how you'd like to leave it. But we're not complete strangers, you know."

His shoulders drooped and he said, "I just don't know how to do this whole dating thing, Karen." Ah, we had something very much in common after all.

Anyone who claims to know how to do this whole dating thing is automatically suspect in my book. Sam came over and gave me a hug.

"Thanks," I said. "And happy New Year, Sam." I meant it. He wished me a happy New Year again, and this time it held at least a whiff of sincerity. It lifted my spirits, as did the knowledge that, thanks to our 6:00 p.m. kickoff, I still had plenty of time to salvage my evening. As soon as I got home, I donned a pair of fuzzy pants, lit a fake log in the fireplace, and put on some Ella Fitzgerald. I basked in the blue-orange glow cast by the flaming pressed wood and in the joy of writing my own happy ending.

# 17

## CATS AND THEIR CLAUSE

As a lawyer and a U.S. citizen, I'm somewhat reluctant to speak harshly of the American legal system. It works twenty-four/seven, spending half its time safeguarding us from potential abuses of government and the other half trying to protect us from our own idiocy. (Our capacity for stupidity must be boundless, judging by my recent purchase of a toaster with a warning label affixed to the back that said: "For indoor use only." C'mon, people. Everyone knows toasters starve in the wild.)

Most of the time the system does a fairly decent job, but it screwed up royally in December of 2012 when it confronted a constitutional issue involving, of all things, cats. The fifty to sixty cats in question live in Key West, Florida, at 907 Whitehead Street. I went to

Key West in January of 2013 to attend a humor workshop, so I took the opportunity to probe further into the case.

I learned that, from 1931 to 1938, Ernest Hemingway lived at 907 Whitehead Street with a cat named Snowball. Poor Snowball started out with two strikes against him. First, he was forced to shack up with the guy who inflicted *The Old Man and the Sea* on an unsuspecting reading population. I haven't read the whole thing but I've read enough of it to know the plot revolves around fishing, which hardly makes for a page-turner. In fact, page turning involves considerably more exertion than your average fishing outing. And this was not your average fishing trip, by the way, because the guy went eighty-five days without catching anything. Who wants to read 127 pages about that? And then, as if sharing a rack with Hemingway weren't insult enough, Snowball was a polydactyl cat, which meant that in addition to the standard set of front paws, he had a pair of non-opposable thumbs.

Eventually the bell tolled for Hemingway and Snowball.

Once Hemingway was out of the picture, the descendants of Snowball (who also had extra digits) saw no reason to leave, so they stuck around and proliferated. In 1964, the house on Whitehead Street effectively became a museum, but the cats, whose ranks had swelled to sixty or so, were never displaced. To this day the museum owners keep and feed the cats and provide them with weekly veterinary care. The owners probably do this out of the goodness of their hearts, but it's also for the goodness of the business: tourists love these furry little six-fingered squatters.

All was well until 2009, when someone who visited the museum expressed concern about the museum's care of the cats to the U.S. Department of Agriculture. To make a very long legal story short, the USDA decided that it had authority to regulate the museum under the Animal Welfare Act, a federal statute. The USDA found its authority in the fact that the cats are "exhibited" to tourists (many of whom come from out of state) and therefore affect interstate commerce and fall within the domain of federal law. The museum responded to the USDA's intervention by filing a class action suit on behalf of crazy cat ladies everywhere. I joke, but only about the class action part. The museum really did file suit, and when it lost at the district court level, it appealed.

And that's how the Eleventh Circuit Court of Appeals found itself presiding over a cat case, which is every jurist's lifelong dream.

The case turned on whether cats chilling at the Hemingway crib while the public tours it amounts to "distribution" of the cats. (The cats, meanwhile, never actually leave the grounds of the house. It's on a choice street in Key West, so why would they?) In its decision, the court shredded the word "distribution" to ribbons on its way to concluding that yes, these cats are distributed and they do, in fact, affect interstate commerce. In other words, these cats aren't just polydactyl; they're constitutional too.

The court must have felt guilty about the little present it dropped in the museum's legal litter box, because it wrote, "Notwithstanding our holding, we appreciate the museum's somewhat unique situation, and we sympathize with its frustration." But that didn't stop them from kicking sand over the whole mess and concluding by saying, "Nevertheless, it is not the court's role to evaluate the wisdom of federal regulations implemented according to the powers constitutionally vested in Congress."

Indeed it is not. They've already got their hands full protecting the citizenry from toasters.

# 18

## A HARE OUT OF PLACE

Last spring I moved to an Arlington neighborhood whose inhabitants do more than pay lip service to the idea of community. People here make a point of getting to know each other and do things like leave welcome gifts for new arrivals. (An unidentified neighbor left me an eggplant, for example. I thought it was a nice gesture, though some readers feared I had been targeted by a produce terrorist.) The neighborhood also has a robust civic association that puts on well-attended, family-friendly events like a Fourth of July parade, a Halloween parade, and an Easter egg hunt.

My next door neighbors, Toni and Scott, are among the people who play the most active roles in making these events happen. They contribute countless hours of their time to help plan and organize. I'm an engaged citizen too, so I contribute juice boxes, which everyone knows are the cornerstone of any close-knit community.

The annual Easter egg hunt was scheduled to take place today, so I stopped by my neighbors' house last night with my contribution. To my standard kid-friendly juice offering I had added a bottle of adult grape juice, which Toni and I proceeded to share. I hadn't seen her in a while, so we had some catching up to do. About-two thirds of the way through the bottle, the topic of conversation shifted to the egg hunt.

"So do you guys have everything you need?" I asked.

"I think we're all set," she said. "We spent two hours stuffing plastic eggs on Monday, so we have enough of those, we have snacks, and we've got juice."

"Sounds like you thought of everything." Knowing Toni, she had.

"Well, except for one thing," she said, taking an ominous pause and a large gulp of wine. "We don't have an Easter bunny." The rabbit makes an appearance at the hunt every year. The neighborhood teenager who usually dons the suit was out of town, leaving a vacancy at a key position in the lineup. "We were hoping maybe a kid who needed some community service hours would do it."

Any job that's described in terms a parole officer would use is bound to be a plum assignment. My wine certainly saw it that way, because it took over the talking and said, "I'll do it."

"Really?" Toni said. "You don't have to, you know."

This did not deter the wine, which said, "Oh, I've done time in an animal suit before, so it's really no big deal." And then it got to bragging about my stints years earlier as a cow mascot in the Peach Bowl. "I've conducted marching bands on national television and done a few commercials," it said. My spoken resume impressed Toni to the point where she didn't feel the need to call my references. I was hired.

The hunt was due to start at 10:00 a.m. at a park a couple of blocks from my house. I showed up at 9:45. Toni passed the suit to me on the sly and I slipped into one of the houses adjacent to the park for my costume change. I was pleased to discover the rabbit outfit weighed a lot less than the cow suit I'd worn before; however, this suit featured the same vision impairment, oxygen deprivation, and unlimited heat that came standard in the other suit. Since I could only see my feet, I knew I needed a handler.

On getting the head further situated, I also realized that one of the eyes had popped out. Unless the neighborhood was prepared to foot dozens of bills for toddler psychotherapy, the suit needed some surgery. The people whose house I was changing in –total strangers to me – lent a glue stick to the cause. Once my eye had been newly adhered, off I went, amid much fanfare. Or so I'm told.

Few things polarize the kid world like life-sized holiday characters. Kids either love 'em or hate 'em. The sight of the Easter bunny caused more than a few kids to burst into tears, judging by the sound of things. Other kids adored me, which I figured out mainly by tripping over them. It warmed my heart to have a fan club.

And, as all self-respecting public figures do, I also had a stalker. One little girl grabbed my paw and started dragging me around the park. When my handler intervened and redirected me, the toddler clung to my leg like a barnacle to a boat. Meanwhile my bum eye had come loose and was flapping in the breeze. This increased the flow of oxygen slightly and the risk of inflicting psychiatric trauma on the kids exponentially. Even with this expanded opening, breathing was still a bit of a struggle, so I spent much of my time tugging on the bunny head to try to align its mouth to my own. After about half an hour, my tour of duty ended. No doubt the civic association was deeply grateful for my services. After all, it's not every day that the neighborhood kids get to see a one-eyed, nose-picking Easter bunny. But I won't be surprised if they ask me to stick with the juice boxes next year.

# 19

## THAT 70 SHOW

On Saturday my father, my siblings, and I threw my mother a surprise party at National Harbor in Maryland to celebrate her seventi-eth birthday. We were joined by aunts and uncles from nearby Waldorf, as well as not-so-nearby Coopersburg, Pennsylvania, and Philadelphia, Mom's hometown.

We kicked off the festivities with dinner at McLoone's Pier House. The restaurant sits right on the waterfront and offers beautiful sunset vistas, especially if you hold up one hand and block out the sight of the nearby Woodrow Wilson Bridge. To lend the gather-ing the gravitas it deserved, Dad had gotten T-shirts made and handed them out as everyone sat down. (We should have handed out sunglasses too, because the afternoon sun poured in through the windows at

McLoone's with an intensity that could have roasted almonds.) Dad's creations were pale blue with maroon writing, a color scheme that honored Mom's beloved Philadelphia Phillies. Our shirts read, "Happy Birthday, Philly's Finest," and the guest of honor's said, "I'm not 70, I'm $69.95 plus tax." We were off to a classy start.

Our family likes to incorporate sporting events or live music into milestone birthday celebrations. When we were planning Mom's bash, we wanted to take her to see Johnny Mathis, one of her favorite singers. Unfortunately, he wasn't coming any closer to D.C. than Atlantic City, and the logistics proved insurmountable. Same with Barry Manilow, another of Mom's faves. At 0–2, we had gotten behind in the cheesy music count but were determined not to strike out. We decided to hold phase two of Mom's party at Bobby McKey's, a piano bar a block and a half from McLoone's. Mom had been to Bobby's once before (for my bachelorette party, of all things), so we felt pretty confident that she'd enjoy herself.

At 7:45 p.m., we marched our team of blue and maroon into the piano bar and up to our seats in the balcony on the second floor. When the show got underway, we began to appreciate just how strategic our position was. We could see the stage perfectly but were far enough away to make the music marginally less likely to explode our eardrums. Also, since the average Bobby McKey's patron looked twenty-five years younger than most of the people in our group, our balcony seats provided a little bit of demographic cover.

The pianists encouraged the crowd to make on-the-spot requests, so I wrote one on a napkin, along with a note about Mom's big birthday. I headed downstairs, walked on stage, and put the request and a $5 bill on the closest piano. My request got played a little while later, and our group sent up a huge cheer. The stage lights kept the pianists from seeing us, but they still made a pretty big fuss about Mom and her seventieth.

"Come on up, Mary Ann!" one of the pianists said as the song ended. But the distance between balcony and stage was too great to cover quickly, so Mom missed her moment. We felt a bit sad about that until we watched the pianists "honor" a few other special guests, who appeared to be bachelorettes and birthday girls in their twenties. The tributes to these gals leaned heavily toward the salty side, so relief replaced our disappointment pretty quickly. An hour and a half later, the pianos were blanketed in cash and requests. A bunch of these must have been aimed at people celebrating birthdays, because the pianists decided to sing the birthday song once to honor all of the birthday girls at one time.

The first pianist had called them all up on stage and was about to launch into the song when he stopped and said, "Hey, what about Mary Ann? Can we get Mary Ann down here?" He looked up toward the balcony. My siblings and I exchanged nervous glances. We looked at Mom, who showed no signs of fear. With a collective shoulder shrug we sent her downstairs for whatever fate awaited. I followed her, in case she needed backup.

As Mom walked on stage, the other pianist looked at her and said, "No way, Mary Ann, you're not seventy," and he had a point: Mom seems much younger than her age in both looks and spirit. Mom's face lit up. Next they called up a few more women, all bachelorettes. They divided the onstage group into four teams of three. Mom's teammates were an African American woman who might have been thirty and a very young, feisty, and intoxicated blonde wearing a bridal veil and an army T-shirt.

Our collective uneasiness increased when we saw the team next to Mom's. One of them held a large, inflatable replica of a male reproductive organ and was swinging it around like a golf club. The pianists then announced that there would be a dance-off. On hearing this, I looked up to the balcony. My siblings were now sitting a little lower in their seats, as if bracing for impact. Mom had come of age during the days of

*American Bandstand* and is a terrific dancer, but having skills like those at a place like Bobby McKey's is like bringing a whiffle bat to a home run derby.

The piano men struck up a tune, and it took me a moment to recognize it, perhaps because it's not every day that you hear a piano rendition of Justin Timberlake's "Sexyback." The pianists had the teams dance to the JT masterpiece for about ten seconds each, beginning with the team farthest away from Mom's. The first two groups bumped and ground in a largely rhythmic fashion. The third team swung their hips and pelvises to a beat only they could hear, augmenting their moves with liberal use of the inflatable prop.

Finally Mom's team was up. I was afraid to watch, and afraid not to. I put a hand over my eye and parted my third and fourth fingers just far enough to give me a tiny glimpse of the stage. Mom and her team did, indeed, bring sexy back. And they gave it a most unexpected traveling companion: dignity. How they did it, I don't know (the two-millimeter window between my fingers gave me a limited field of vision), but all three of them kept their moves cute, classy, and restrained. And any worries we had about how our mother might get treated were put to rest when the crowd, which voted with applause, went wild for Mom and her team. Their performance netted them a berth in the finals with two other teams. (The golfing girls didn't make it to the big dance, proving that the crowd was a pretty good arbiter of taste after all.)

According to my sister, when my brother heard this news, he leaned over and deadpanned, "Well, it's Mom's to lose now." And sure enough, when the time came, Mom and her partners took their sexy dignity and turned it up a notch, leaving the competition in the dust. Mom's teammates hugged her, and the crowd loved it. Victory was theirs. Some hard-fought contest wins come with prizes, but this one came only with bragging rights, and that was perfectly all right by me.

"Hey, that's my mom up there," I said to the people around me, beaming with pride as they applauded and cheered.

# 20

## BRING IN THE POM SQUAD

I'm childless by choice, but I adore being an aunt. When the occasional opportunity arises to pinch hit and play Rent-A-'Rent to my niece and nephews, I always seize it. My sister Lynne and her husband had planned a five-day trip to the Dominican Republic, so I volunteered to help get the kids to and from various activities while the parents were away.

"Great," my sister said. "Can you take Emily to Virginia Beach for her cheer competition?"

On the list of things I don't leave my area code for, a cheerleading showdown ranks way up there, just behind baby showers. I was a tomboy, so cheerleading wasn't on my radar when I was a kid. The sports I played then (and still play now) involved dirt, water,

113

and balls, not quantities of makeup best described as "bridal." But since I support everything my niece does, I made an exception to my longstanding policy and signed up to chauffeur and chaperone her trip to the U.S. Cheer and Dance Finals.

In the short time that Emily has been cheering, I have come to appreciate that this is a serious athletic pursuit, lip gloss and high ponies notwithstanding. I've watched her and her friends handspring all the way across a floor mat, do leaping toe touches (the very idea of which sends my back into vicarious spasms), and launch each other into the air while maintaining a pyramid formation. If you're a skeptic who still has to be convinced that cheering isn't some frivolous little hobby, just check out the website for the competition. It's got a countdown, a bellwether of seriousness that puts it in the company of landmark events like New Year's Eve in Times Square and NASA launches. Using those as my guide, I decided to bring booze and strap in.

Like most events, the Cheer and Dance Finals had its pluses and minuses. On the positive side, it gave me a rare chance to spend a lot of one-on-one time with Emily, whose sunny disposition and laid-back personality make her one of my very favorite people on the planet. Those qualities also make her the only person in the galaxy who could get me to drive four hundred miles to watch her and a dozen of her girlfriends perform a three-minute cheer routine.

Turning to the minuses, nothing in my forty-one-year existence could have prepared me for the sights, sounds, and smells I experienced at the cheerleading finals on Saturday. After parking the car and forking over $20 for admission, I walked through the doors of the Virginia Beach Convention Center and straight into high-pony Hell. The sight of hundreds of very young girls wearing more makeup than clothing might have alarmed me if I hadn't immediately gotten high on secondhand hairspray fumes. I found Emily's team after a few minutes of dazed wandering.

Clad in long-sleeved fitted shirts, miniskirts, and bloomers, hers was among the most conservatively dressed teams. But they were locked in a dead heat with the other teams when it came to cosmetics. I was told that heavy makeup is needed to make the girls' eyes "pop" because the judges at these competitions aren't very close to the stage. Based on the amount of eye shadow and liner our girls were wearing, the judges must have been sitting in the Mars Rover.

Moments after my arrival, the coaches took our team to a warm-up area, leaving the adults free to watch the teams performing before ours. A couple of these teams left me slack-jawed. It wasn't their lifts and stunts that got me but rather their uniforms, which consisted of open-shouldered belly shirts and hot pants, and their dance moves, which featured more pelvic thrusts than a Britney Spears video. These groups made my niece and her pals look like Team Convent.

Much as I like the fitness and team aspects of cheer, the aesthetic stuff gives me serious pause. But nothing held me back when our team of sweet, beautiful little girls took the stage. They put their hearts into their routine, and we adults gave it our all as we rooted for them. Not everything went as rehearsed—a couple of lifts suddenly became drops—yet our girls never let on that anything was amiss. They didn't falter or stop, and they looked like they were having fun. If nothing else, that kind of perseverance is something to cheer about.

# 21

## YOU HAVE THE RIGHT TO REMAIN SILENT

To celebrate my dad's seventy-first birthday, Mom and I decided to take him to dinner at a nice French restaurant near Occoquan, Virginia, about ten miles south of where my folks live.

As we drove across the Occoquan River, Dad glanced in the rearview mirror, made eye contact with me in the backseat and said, "Remember how I got a ticket here, and you kept me out of jail?" Oh, did I ever. The incident in question happened in 2004, roughly two years after I passed the Virginia bar exam. I knew that getting my law degree would mean requests for free legal advice, but I hadn't expected one of the first ones to come from my father. He'd called me at work one Tuesday morning.

"I got a goddamned speeding ticket, Wheat!" he spat out, disgusted. (Some people call their lawyers "counselor," but not my father. He called me by the childhood nickname I was given thanks to the color and texture of my hair.) I snorted in surprise and then tried to disguise it by coughing. You see, over time, my siblings and I had detected a change in Dad's driving habits. As his age increased, his pressure on the gas pedal had begun to decrease to the point where we were no longer certain he would successfully summit a speed bump. A speeding ticket was nothing short of a major accomplishment.

I said, "Really?" but my tone conveyed an inappropriate level of excitement. "I mean, sorry, Dad. That's unbelievable. How did it happen?"

"It pisses me off just thinking about it." Curse words were one of the surest ways to gauge Dad's passion on any given topic. I'd already counted two, so I knew this was serious. "I was driving on Route 123, crossing over the Occoquan, and that son of a bitch was sitting at the bottom of the hill, just waiting for me. The bastard said I was doing fifty-five in a thirty-five, can you imagine?" I'd been in the car with Dad plenty of times and no, I could not imagine. "You wanna know the worst part?"

"What's that, Dad?"

"Not only will I get socked with a fine, I'll have six points on my license!" Now he really had my attention. My father and I both knew that momentum had caused him to speed, not flagrant disregard for the law.

"Do you think I should fight it?"

"No, Dad. It's a loser unless the cop doesn't show up. But I bet you could get the offense changed so that you pay a higher fine but get fewer points on your license."

And that single piece of advice is how I ended up representing my father in traffic court. Because I'd sounded so confident when I counseled Dad, I couldn't let on that I knew nothing whatsoever about how to carry out my advice. I didn't even know how to enter my appearance on Dad's behalf.

When the day of my father's hearing arrived, I was more than a little nervous. Dad, Mom, and I met outside of the Fairfax County Courthouse, an overly quaint name for a building that's the size of a major shopping mall. It took me fifteen minutes to figure out how to enter the building, which did not bode well for my hopes of entering an appearance. After bumbling around for a bit I managed to find the courtroom and to fill out the representation form correctly. Things were looking up.

We entered the courtroom where, right away, I saw two people I knew. Even better, neither was a defendant. In fact, both were practicing attorneys who appeared in court regularly, one a friend of a friend from work (he'd served with my friend's husband in Iraq), and the other my sister Lynne's divorce lawyer. Surely one guy who managed to escape a war zone unscathed and another who got my sister unmarried had figured out how to conquer traffic court. And, as luck would have it, the two were sitting a few feet apart from each other in the same pew. I leaned forward, inserted my head between them, and quietly re-introduced myself. Each registered mild surprise but the Marine recovered first.

"Holy smokes, I haven't seen you since you started law school."

"You went to law school?" the divorce lawyer said. "Wow, do you have a client here?" I explained the situation. They turned around, glanced at Dad, and shook their heads in joint disbelief. They were ready to help. At their suggestion, I approached the prosecutor during a break in cases and cut a deal for "failure to pay time and attention," an offense that carried a heftier fine but zero points on the license. When our case was called, Dad and I made our way forward to the defense table.

I turned to him and whispered, "Don't say anything unless I tell you to. I'll do the talking here."

"I can't believe it. My own daughter telling me to shut up." But that was the extent of his resistance.

I entered my appearance for the record, getting only slightly hung up when forced to refer to my father as "the defendant." The prosecutor told the judge what we'd agreed upon. As the judge asked Dad if that was the plea he wanted to enter, my father looked at me for permission to speak. I nodded.

"Yes," he said. Upon uttering that lone syllable, our case was done, and all Dad had to do was write a check. As soon as we left the courtroom, he reached for my hand. A handshake? He seemed to be taking this whole attorney–client thing a bit too seriously. But instead of shaking my hand, Dad pressed something into it and closed my fingers around it. I opened my hand to find a $50 bill. Had he just greased my palm?

"What's this for, Dad?"

"You know, today," he said. And then he gave me a wink that would have made Don Corleone proud. Fantastic. Dad had beaten the six-point rap and I'd just been given the world's crappiest retainer. But nearly a decade later, he's still my partner in crime.

# 22

## YOU'VE COME A LONG WAY, BABY

I approach beaches the same way I do wine: I accept
whatever I'm offered with gratitude, but I definitely have preferences. I like a beach that isn't overly
commercial and doesn't have a boardwalk. And I want
it to have real, pounding surf that doesn't care how
messy it looks when it lands, instead of those ankle-
biter waves that are so prissy and timid they practically
ask permission to come ashore.

I owe my taste in beaches to my family's summer vacations in the Outer Banks of North Carolina. We spent
a week there every summer when I was a kid, starting
when I was six. In those days, the Outer Banks were
quite rustic. The beach offered the lone source of entertainment, and it was more than enough. During the

day, we rode the waves in inner tubes, body-surfed, and made sand castles. At night, we strolled the sand armed with flashlights and a net, hoping to snag the crabs that sometimes rolled in with the tide. We slept soundly, the roaring waves easing us into our dreams more effectively than any lullaby I've heard before or since. We loved it there, and it has always felt like home to me.

When I decided to go away to write a few weekends ago, the Outer Banks sprang to mind as the perfect destination. For maximum inspirational effect, I splurged and booked an oceanfront room at the Hilton Garden Inn in Kitty Hawk. That whole transaction felt a little strange to me because when I was a kid, the town didn't even have a chain hotel, much less a five-story one. Not that my family ever would have stayed in a place like that anyway.

Back in the day, a friend of my father's owned a beach house in Kitty Hawk, and that's where we spent our vacations. Actually, let me back up, because "house" is a bit of an overstatement. The Beach Baby, as the house was known, began her life as a two-car garage that belonged to the home next door. Cars demanded less space back then, so this garage wasn't one of those twenty-four-foot-wide jobs that you see today. Nor did it have extra space for bikes, woodworking, or any other garage frivolities. It was built for exactly one purpose: to house two cars.

Eventually someone whose real estate vision was better than 20/20 came along and saw that it would make great sense to convert the oceanfront garage into an oceanfront house. This person understood that some changes would be needed to make the structure habitable, seeing as how humans' and cars' needs for indoor plumbing sometimes differ. He started by adding a full bathroom. And that's also where he stopped, because there was no need to go off on some crazy square footage binge.

Into the two-car garage with a bathroom, the visionary then packed a fridge, a small counter and stove, a table and chairs, a set of bunk beds, two twin beds, a full bed, and a dresser. If you're trying to picture the sleeping configuration and asking yourself how in the world all five beds fit into the space of a one-car garage, the answer is: they didn't. The full bed was in the kitchen. This offered a certain convenience, especially for the kind of person who wakes up at 2:00 a.m. craving yesterday's potato salad but doesn't want to leave the bed to get it. The full bed also boasted a short commute to the bathroom, though you couldn't get there just by sitting up. You had to walk up a couple of steps near the foot of the bed. Those steps weren't placed there for aesthetic effect; they were a necessity so the bathroom door could be opened without smacking into the kitchen bed.

If you're impressed by the way the Beach Baby raised the efficiency concept to new heights, don't be, because she was a real inefficiency when it came to time. With six people and only one bathroom, someone had to be showering at every waking moment if we had any hopes of going out to dinner before midnight. The people-to-bathroom ratio also meant that bodily functions weren't mandates so much as requests that you did your best to honor, assuming you could find a four-minute window when someone wasn't in the shower. But what the Beach Baby lacked in amenities she more than compensated for with location: she sat right smack dab on the beach. If you stepped out the back door, you were standing on sand, and high tide was never more than a few yards away.

We weren't the only ones who loved the Beach Baby's location. Mother Nature did too. She's quite the real estate visionary herself, and she had big plans for the Beach Baby. When hurricane season was in full swing one year in the mid-1980s, Mother Nature took the garage-turned-house and turned it into a fully furnished raft.

The Beach Baby is gone now, and has been for a long time. But she still lives on in our memories...and who knows where else.

# 23

## SLEEP NUMBERS

Insomnia has dogged me for pretty much my whole life. In college and law school I saw it as an advantage because it gave me hours of potentially productive time that other people wasted sawing logs. But I haven't been in school for over a decade, and during that time the insomnia has only gotten worse. Add middle age to the equation and you get a person whose sleep pattern is like an NFL game: three or four hours long with constant, pointless interruptions. When I wake up for good, usually around 4:00 a.m., I feel fine. But by 9:00 a.m., I'm fighting urges to nod off while doing normal daytime activities, like operating a chain saw. A good friend who stayed with me recently couldn't help but notice my sleeping habits, and they worried him.

"You can't get by on three or four hours a night," he said, citing a litany of long-term health risks like stroke, high blood pressure, and heart failure. I was moved by his concern and about to say as much when he added, "And I can hear you snore through the walls." Nothing will get an unattached female to seek medical attention faster than telling her she sleeps like Homer Simpson.

I called a nearby hospital's sleep lab and made an intake appointment. During the consultation, the doctor, who of course was young and attractive, asked questions about my sleep habits and managed not to snicker when I got to the part about snoring the walls down. He declared me a good sleep study candidate and gave me a brief overview of the process. As he described it, all I had to do was spend a night at the hospital in a room that he assured me had all the trappings of a double at the Holiday Inn. The lab staff would collect data while I snoozed.

"Once we do the study," he said, "we should know a lot more about why you're not sleeping. And if your issues stem from sleep apnea, like many people's do, then these could solve your problems." He gestured to a tray. It held a mask that bore a striking resemblance to the one worn by Hannibal Lecter in *Silence of the Lambs*, along with several other libido busters masquerading as sleep disorder treatment devices. I was warming up to the idea of heart failure.

"I know I already mentioned this," I said, "but I'm single. Do you have any idea what that would do to my dating life?" I pointed at the mask.

"Oh, don't worry, you don't have to get that one," he said. "You can get one with a pink nose." Oh good. Instead of Hannibal Lecter, I could look like Petunia Pig. The appliance to which the mask connects is the size of a toaster, another bonus. Few things jazz up the décor of a bedroom like the presence of a hosed-up toaster on the nightstand.

The doctor's staff scheduled me for a study and handed me a packet of instructions on how to prepare for it. These included patently nonsensical mandates like "Do not consume caffeine or alcohol on the day of your study," along with more reasonable ones, like "Wear clothes." Let's face it: the last thing the hospital needs is a bunch of streakers, even if the sleep lab is right next door to the trauma unit.

I followed the instructions to the letter and showed up for the study at 9 p.m. on a Sunday evening. The waiting area was crowded with adults clutching pillows, blankets, and other sleeping paraphernalia. I felt like an extra in the slumber party scene from *Grease*. I was soon ushered to a private room that contained a double bed with decent linens. It could have passed easily for a room at the Holiday Inn, especially if you sprang for the "Wires All Over Your Person" package. For just a few extra bucks, a technician affixes electrodes to every exposed surface on your body except your eyebrows. And then he tells you to go ahead and nod off whenever you feel like it, a perfectly natural thing to do when you are festooned with wires.

Eventually I must have fallen asleep. I remember being woken up to reattach something that fell off, and then waking for good at 4:45 a.m. It had been an uneventful, if not relaxing, night.

After mentioning the sleep study in a blog post I wrote, I took my time writing up the results. Several people who noticed that my appointment date had come and gone started to ask me about it, in rather impatient tones. None of them came right out and said, "You're up for half the night, WHY THE HELL DON'T YOU WRITE THE FLIPPING BLOG?!?," but I could tell they were thinking it.

I soon figured out what was driving their acute interest in my sleep. It wasn't so much that they were worried about my wellbeing as they were hoping for some new weapons to deploy in the Global War On Spousal Snoring. Since I'm nothing if not an expert on all things marital, I was delighted to be of service.

When I went back to see the doctor, he handed me a report that contained my sleep study stats, which did not add up to apnea:

- Time in the bed: 419 min
- Time sleeping: 259 min (62%)
- REM sleep total: 36 min (14%)
- Time awake after sleep onset: 117 min
- Number of "arousals": 79 (If you immediately thought, "Well no *wonder* she's up all night," this is nowhere near as romantic as it sounds. "Arousals" is a polite term for snoring yourself awake.)
- No limb movements
- No cardiac arrhythmias
- Heart rate while awake: 47.5 BPM
- Heart rate while asleep: 47 BPM

After walking me through the numbers, the doctor said, "Your sleep architecture doesn't indicate a physiological issue beyond snoring." Maybe not, but I'm pretty sure any building with that architecture would be condemned.

I said, "Don't get me wrong, I'm thrilled to hear I won't have to wear that mask …but what do I do now?"

"Oh, don't worry," he said, all smiles and reassurance. "There's a new product that treats the snoring. If you can manage not to disrupt your sleep in the first place, then your problem of being awake for long periods might solve itself."

This sounded great as he started telling me about the product, which is basically a set of high-tech adhesives that go under your nostrils. The adhesive has mesh that allows you to inhale through your nose but forces you to exhale through your mouth, thereby ensuring that your airway stays open.  I was looking forward to solving my problems with nothing more than fancy nose stickers as the doctor handed me the product literature. A photo on the front depicted a woman in a state of restful slumber, wearing the nose stickers and looking quite relaxed for someone who appears to have snorted a butterfly.

On seeing my reaction, he shifted topics and began to describe different techniques I could use to try to slow my racing mind. He mentioned progressive muscle relaxation, where you start at your toes and do a flex/stretch combination that you repeat as you slowly travel up your body. This might work for people who have normal minds, but I'm pretty sure mine wouldn't make it past my knees before it got distracted and started singing "Dem Bones."

The doctor suggested a second technique called creative imagery, which involves mentally sending yourself to a specific happy location from your childhood. Maybe a few mental trips to the Outer Banks will eventually send me to Dreamland.

# 24

## THE ARM CHARM MANIFESTO

It's happened to pretty much all of us at some point in our adult lives: you get invited to a date function when you're between relationships. You find yourself going through your contacts in search of the "Arm Charm": the utterly platonic pal who cleans up well enough to be seen with in public and probably won't burp the alphabet at dinner. My good friend Mike got an invitation a few months ago to a wedding in Mason, Ohio, and needed a date. He asked if I was up for it.

"My bags are packed!" I said, what with Mike being a close friend and with Mason being second only to Maui on TheKnot.com's list of Top 10 Wedding Destinations.

As we were making our way to the Rust Belt for the wedding, I gave some thought to how to be a good Arm Charm and came up with the following list of rules.

- **<u>Do NOT dance like nobody's watching</u>.** The wedding of a friend twice removed is not the time to live out a commencement speech cliché, no matter how close you are to perfecting your human dreidel impression.

- **<u>Know your personality</u>.** You probably think I'm referring to the Myers-Briggs personality test. That can be important, but you must also take inventory of your Absolut personality. If you don't, and you fail to regulate your drink intake properly, you might make the abrupt and unfortunate transition from I-N-F-P to A-R-S-E.

- **<u>Don't be selfish</u>.** The Airplane Oxygen Mask Rule does not apply when you're the Arm Charm. You're there to help your date first and foremost, which means you don't abandon him to go hit on the Channing Tatum lookalike at the next table. This one sprang to mind based on an experience I had in 2008. My then-boyfriend dumped me the day before my fifteen-year college reunion, leaving me dateless at the last minute. I called my usual sub dude, a known violator of "Do NOT dance like nobody's watching" but otherwise a reliable Arm Charm. To my great relief, he was only too happy to fill in. At one of the reunion events, I sent him off to get me a drink, an errand that should have taken two minutes. When ten minutes had passed and he was nowhere in sight, I headed to the bar in the name of self-help. My friend had also engaged in self-help, which I discovered when I spotted him across the room, smooching one of my classmates.

- **If you see something, say something.** The same guidance we use to report suspicious activity to the government applies to anything that makes your date look bad. Don't let him walk around with a stray hair hanging out of his nose like a garter snake.

- **Clean up your act.** When you're the Arm Charm, you have to bring your "A" game, appearance wise. Dudes, this means shaving that hair kudzu that grows on the back of your neck. Ladies, if you're wearing open-toed shoes, you have to paint your toenails. At least the visible ones.

If you're wondering how I fared last weekend in practicing what I preached, let's just say four out of five ain't bad.

# 25

## WHO NEEDS A HUSBAND, ANYWAY?

My friend Philippa had breast cancer surgery in the fall of 2013, and I stayed with her during the post-op recovery period. Philippa knew that my idea of nursing involved leaving a cocktail unattended for too long, so I asked her why she picked me for this post. Was it two decades of close friendship? My tender, nurturing side?

"It's your insomnia," she said. My chronic inability to sleep apparently made me the perfect person to administer drugs at all hours. I'm as susceptible to flattery as the next person so I wasted no time accepting the nomination and began to plan for my stint as the embedded friend. My pre-op due diligence included talking to another close friend who recently underwent a similar surgery and asking her for caregiving suggestions.

"Ya gotta let her whine a little bit," my pal said, "like maybe five minutes a day." It seemed like good advice, even after she told me I had to let unused minutes roll over like on a cell phone plan.

Though we had to dedicate portions of every day to medical issues, the patient and I spent enormous amounts of time laughing. We did it not because we think cancer is funny, or because we underestimate it. We did it precisely *because* it's terrifying and overwhelming. Laughter gave us a way to wrest a modicum of control from a disease whose power requires no explanation. Laughter helped us pass the agonizing wait for the return of the pathology results. And it brought healing from physical and psychological trauma, except when Philippa laughed so hard that it engaged her chest muscles in a medically un-recommended way. A whopping dose of humor might not have been what everyone would want in that situation, but it's what my friend wanted and I was glad to contribute.

In the weeks leading up to Philippa's surgery, support poured in from all kinds of sources, including women she'd never met who'd had breast cancer. These amazing ladies offered her a unique and vital kind of empathy. And they flooded her with pragmatic post-surgery advice and gear. One of these newfound friends knew that the surgical drains make it difficult to rest, so she handed off what Philippa described as "a big pillow with two arm thingies."

Based on her description I knew exactly what it was and said, "Oh, that's a husband." Philippa cracked up. "What's so funny?" I asked.

"I locked my husband in the trunk," she said. Eventually we took the husband out of the trunk and let him hang around the condo during Philippa's recovery.

Like husbands the world over, this one proved a bottomless source of material. Because Philippa and I are both happily divorced, we didn't feel any urge to get too close to the husband, but we liked him a lot anyway. Here's why:

- He didn't argue. At most he put up a tiny bit of resistance before submitting.
- If we gave him shelter, he was happy. He didn't make any other demands.
- He didn't care if I'd been in bed with someone else.
- He appreciated it when I took him places and never criticized my driving, my taste in music, or my climate management.

- He never made me late.
- He wouldn't push me out of bed even if I'd had garlic fries with garlic aioli and a side of roasted garlic for dinner.
- He was perfectly content to sit at home in the corner while I hung out with the girls.
- Seeing me parade around naked didn't make him act all crazy.
- He seemed to understand that, while I was glad to have borrowed him and might someday like him enough to want one of my own, I got along just fine without him.

# 26

## LINE 'EM UP

Your friend lineup—the list of nonfamily types you really count on—has to include people of the opposite gender, regardless of whether you're male or female, gay or straight, single or married. These people fill a vital perspective gap, at the very least, and they often do much more than that. For example, while caring for my friend Philippa after she underwent a double mastectomy, I watched as her guy friends did things like drive her to the hospital, make her smoothies, keep her stocked up on flowers, and whip up a delectable Bolognese.

The experience brought me fresh appreciation for my man friends ("The Dudes") and the realization that there are certain guy-friend types that I simply can't live without. Without further ado, I bring you my very own personal Dude Roster:

**The Sub Dude:** Your "plus one" when you need a date, this purely platonic pal adheres to the Arm Charm Manifesto, keeps you entertained, and is socially savvy enough to know when to give you a little space. Bonus points if he looks smokin' in a tux.

**The Sidekick:** This guy is equal parts fun, fearless, and adventurous. He's the dude you want riding shotgun when you make a last-minute decision to road trip. Or when you need a guest cohost for your podcast, hypothetically.

**The Work Hubs:** This husband hasn't seen you parade around the house wearing nose stickers, but you and he work so closely that he's witnessed the office equivalent and he still likes you. Most of the time.

**The Flagman:** Like the guy who halts traffic for roadwork, the Flagman points out hazards you might not be able to see and tries his best to get you to slow down or, in extreme cases, detour. My friend and co-worker, Alan, does this for me. He earned the job as a result of some doodling he did on a whiteboard one day while

I was telling him about a date I'd gone on the night before. As I yammered on about how my date was basically nice except for his tendency to bring up exes who seemed unable to get over him, Alan busied himself drawing a red-triangular thing that sat atop what appeared to be a pole.

"Do you recognize this?" Alan said.

"It looks like the pin for the eighteenth hole on a golf course."

"Nope," he said, shaking his head. "It's just as I feared, Karen. You can't see what this is because you have Red Flag Detection Disorder. Best-case scenario, this guy's insecure and has an endless need to have women adore him and to make sure you know it. Worst-case scenario, he's not over his ex. Either way, do NOT go out with this man again." I did not heed Alan's advice, of course, but a second date proved him right.

**The Broker:** This dude traffics not in financial instruments but in honesty. About everything. It's critical to have at least one of these on hand at all times, preferably two or three. The Broker, for example, will tell you what he really thinks of your clothing choices. He's one of very few people who won't treat "Does my butt look big in these pants?" as rhetorical. I once posed a variant of this question to my friend Joseph and he said, "Hmmm...if butts were states, those pants don't make yours look like Texas, but it ain't Rhode Island either."

I would be lost without the Dudes, whose presence in my life reminds me on a regular basis that everybody needs a few good men.

# 27

## TOES IN THE WATER

My friend Philippa and I recently wrote posts in which we gushed about our guy friends. She said she's got such great guy friends that it would be almost impossible for her to date anyone seriously. I know what she means. I have an armada of awesome dude pals, too, but that's not the reason I've spent most of the past two years on the dating sidelines. I just hadn't been ready to attempt a relationship. But it's been a year and a half since I finalized my divorce, and it's time for me to get serious about Meeting Someone.

Don't get me wrong, I've met men just by doing stuff I enjoy—hanging out with friends, taking trips, playing sports, and going to various events—but most of them haven't been available. I decided a more targeted approach was in order: online dating. I soon learned that the online dating world is vast, and there are sites for practically every age, preference, and interest group. I even discovered sites for inmates and the people who want to date them (inmate.com and WomenBehindBars.com).

An article reviewed these two prison dating sites and noted, on the plus side, that "[m]ost of the ads include the prisoner's release date, so you can make long-term plans." Because, really, no one wants a gap in life sentences. Since every pro has a con (ha!), the review criticized the sites because they don't provide much information about the crimes. If you ask me, this omission makes perfect sense. Seasoned daters know that details of your conviction are second date material at the earliest.

Anyway, given the sheer number of sites available, I didn't know how to choose, so I consulted one of my guy friends who's done multiple tours of duty in the online dating trenches. He's smart, attractive, funny, and roughly my age, so I trust him. He suggested PlentyOfFish.com because, based on his experience, the male-to-female ratio there was at least five to one. Since the odds in D.C. are practically the opposite, those numbers were reason enough to check out POF. Before you can cast a line on POF, you have to create a profile by answering a series of questions. I was cruising down the virtual dating superhighway, answering easy questions like "Smoker? Y/N," when I ran smack into a jersey wall: body type.

POF lists five categories: thin, athletic, average, a few extra pounds, and big and tall. I'm a bit over 5'7" and weigh 130 pounds, plus or minus four depending on the prior day's chocolate intake. On a height/weight chart, this puts me at the lower end of normal, so I didn't know whether to choose "thin" or "normal." Since I also swim, play tennis, run, and do boot camp, I decided that choosing "athletic" would be an elegant solution to the dilemma. I bragged about my savvy to Philippa over dinner at our favorite Italian joint last night.

Red wine practically erupted out of her as she said, "Wait, you chose 'athletic'? No, no, no, no, no! Don't you know this is all code? 'Athletic' doesn't mean you're fit! It means the Bears drafted you in the second round. YOU HAVE TO CHANGE IT!" I did. And then I posted a photo, specifically a very flattering picture that my sister snapped during our trip to South Beach last fall.

With that, my submission was complete. Now let's see if I get any bites.

# 28

## THE GREATEST HITS

Regular readers know that I play on a women's tennis team called the Smash Hits. The Smashes, as I refer to them, are a terrific group of ladies ranging in age from twenty-five to seventy, and one of them just happens to be my mom. I joined the team in April 2012, when I was in the middle of a move and would have done just about anything to avoid unpacking. A year and a half later, the Smashes made me their captain. I'd like to tell you that I earned the job through stellar play, but the truth is that I lost a bet. As captain, I manage the schedule, set the lineup, and report the results of every match.

Our league is organized by the United States Tennis Association, which has a ranking system that's used to group players, teams, and leagues based on skill. The USTA scale ranges from 1.5 to 7.0, where 1.5 means "knows the difference between a tennis racquet and a pool stick" and 7.0 means "Rafael Nadal." The USTA has pronounced the Smash Hits a 3.0 team. Despite our fair-to-middling ranking, the Smashes are formidable, racquet-wielding gladiators, as evidenced by our team motto: "If you can't be good, look good."

Based on our motto, you may have inferred that the Smashes tend to lose at least as often as we win. You would not be wrong. I'm not saying we aren't competitive, but our collective killer instinct is more likely to come out in the shoe section at Nordstrom than on the tennis court. We use team meetings not to discuss how we might improve our play but to decide on an official team wine (Cupcake Chardonnay).

Since it's my unofficial job to keep team morale high, I work especially hard at writing upbeat match reports after a defeat. Early on in my first season as captain, I got into the habit of writing post-loss reports using the good news/bad news format, thinking I'd never struggle to find something positive to say. And I was right, at least at first. But as the season progressed the "L"s piled up, and finding positive things to report started getting harder. After another difficult loss last week, I sent a team-wide e-mail proclaiming the following good news:

- All eight of our players showed up at the right courts at the right time, eclipsing our previous record of six. Way to go! This was an especially impressive feat, considering that CeCe ran over her tennis racquet.

- We got a really great space in the club parking lot!

We did pick up a win or two along the way, including a 3-1 victory against a team called the Toss-Ups, but even that one came down to the wire. The decisive match in that contest—one in which I happened to play—was won in a tiebreak, and the winning point in the tiebreak came when the other team served up a double-fault. No one wants to win that way, but both my partner and I called the second serve as we saw it: out. The other team didn't like that call, or several others, apparently. We realized this only after the match had ended and, instead of shaking hands, they handed us coupons for a free visit to MyEyeDr. In sum, when we've won, it hasn't been pretty. The regular season ended in early December and we found ourselves in seventh place. Out of eight. Having produced such lackluster results, I felt certain the Smashes were going to fire me, so I began to work on my resume.

All talk of personnel changes evaporated when the league coordinator sent an e-mail informing me that the

Smashes had made it into the postseason. As it turns out, all eight teams reached the playoffs, which pretty much made them play-alls, but I didn't care. We had just three days to prepare for post-season play, which barely gave us time to shop for a playoff uniform, much less practice.

The Smashes and I showed up Friday night at the Four Seasons tennis facility in Fairfax to take on the #2 team, the Ms. Hits, in the first round of the play-offs. Excitement was high and expectations were low. Anyone who plays sports knows that this combination is precisely what makes underdogs so dangerous. To the astonishment of everyone on the courts, and I mean everyone, we beat the Ms. Hits and landed on most unfamiliar terrain: the semifinals.

We returned to Four Seasons three nights later to take on Lots of Lob. I stayed on the sidelines this time. My mind was already on the match report, and watching the matches gave me an idea. As a blogger, I'm on a constant quest for easy content. As captain of the Smashes, I'm always looking for new and entertaining ways to write match reports. I realized I could kill two creative birds with one stone by writing a match report modeled after Clement C. Moore's "A Visit From Saint Nick."

This combination proved better in concept than reality, much like every blind date I've ever been on. The first few lines came to me easily, allowing me to forget that the original poem is FIFTY-TWO LINES LONG. That's as many lines of poetry as there are weeks in the year. Isn't this a bit much for a pagan holiday paean? If you ask me, this could easily have been dealt with via haiku.

*Red-suited fat guy*

*Breaks and enters by chimney*

*Ho ho hum, I say.*

But I forged ahead, enduring forgotten couplets like that one about wild leaves getting hurled into the sky by hurricane-force gales, and weaving in bits of team history where I could. Without further ado, I bring you the report from the semifinals:

*'Twas the night before Finals, when I and the Smashes*

*Went from seventh to semis—a phoenix from ashes.*

*Our rackets had hung by the chimney, whose fires*

KAREN YANKOSKY

*Posed less of a hazard than CeCe's front tires.*

*The ladies had settled into their bathtubs,*

*Where visions of aces replaced those of flubs.*

*Mom donned a helmet because, though off-court,*

*She knows life, just like tennis, is a contact sport.*

*When out at Four Seasons spread all kinds of rumors:*

*"Who are these Smash Hits? Where'd they buy those bloomers?"*

*We walked on the courts with the cool poise of Federer,*

*And with serves just as good as Nadal's, if not betterer.*

*The lights cast a glow, oh so faint, from above*

*That I wanted to yell, "Buy new bulbs, for the love!"*

*When what to my wondering eyes should show up,*

*But Cupcake white wine, in a red sippy cup.*

*(As captain, I now and then turn to the sauce.*

*It cheers when we win and it soothes after loss.)*

*More rapid than eagles, far cuter they came,*

*My eight Smashes. I hooted and called them by name.*

*"Margie, Kate, Telma, Betsey, and Leticia,*

*Mary Beth, 'Becca, and CeCe and Lisa,*

*From the top of your stick to the soles of your shoes,*

*Remember my motto: 'Don't come home if you lose!'"*

*As high-seed teams into the post-season sailed,*

*By my Smashes they were most abruptly derailed.*

*To the L bracket, down all those top teams they went.*

*"Who designed your cute unis?" they asked on descent.*

*Last night I watched, eyes and ears trained with aplomb.*

*What was that on court two, did I hear an F-bomb?*

*As I sucked in my breath and lowered my head*

*My face had the hue sometimes called cherry red.*

*My girls, with demure skirts and tops made by tailors,*

*Can curse with the skill seen most often in sailors.*

*A bundle of games that pair lost in a minute.*

*What the F\*&^ was their deal, weren't they trying to win it?*

*My Smashes, they huddled. I knew they were plannin'*

*And the next serves they hit were shot straight from a cannon.*

*Ready to strike, coiled up like a snake,*

*They claimed the first set without need for tiebreak.*

*All four matches were close, a nail biter for sure.*

*Or would have been, but for my French manicure.*

*The tension, it hung, palpable as a noose.*

*I tried to think happy: Kevin Bacon, Footloose?*

*My Smashes leaned in as the going got tough.*

*They gave it their all, which was more than enough.*

*"Forget the score," I said. "It's as mad as a hatter.*

*All those numbers and letters, are they really what matter?"*

*When the clock struck eleven, we still didn't know—*

*Tied up, two matches each. Where's the chart for that flow?*

*To decide: Total games? Sets? Quadratic equation?*

*I'm a lawyer: From all math I take a vacation.*

*I turned to my girls, to my team gave a tally,*

*Then away they all flew, like line drives down the alley.*

*They shouted, while flooring it, tires all burns,*

*"Merry Christmas, dear Smashes, and blazing returns!"*

The league coordinator wrote the next morning to tell me the decision came down to the total number of games won, which meant the Smashes lost. As I relayed the news to the team, I reminded them that it doesn't matter whether you win or lose: it's how you look on the court. And they looked Smashing.

# 29

## ALL WRAPPED UP IN TRADITION

Christmas tradition doesn't exactly enslave the Yanks, but there are a bunch of things we do as a tribe every holiday season. It would take me weeks to report on how all of our traditions fared this year, so I'll provide a rundown of the top three:

1. Christmas tree cutting: Big thumbs-up. We'd been going to the same farm in Round Hill, a little town in the northern tip of Virginia, for the past several seasons, but last year we began to see signs that perhaps we ought to make a change. First, the farm seemed to have embarked on an ad campaign, because the parking lot the weekend after Thanksgiving had a higher car count as your average Walmart. On top of that, the tree farmers had gone a bit too far in their efforts to diversify their portfolio. They started

out innocuously years ago by selling hot cider in addition to trees. Soon they expanded to selling cookies and pies. By this time last year, they'd added an organic butcher, three vintners, and a nine-piece band. It felt as rustic as Costco. And then there was the matter of transporting our freshly cut trees from field to car, a distance of half a mile or so. If you're not familiar with the experience, carrying an eight-foot felled pine is like handling a ninety-pound cactus. You'd think the farm would help with this part of the process, but you'd be wrong. For $100, not only do you get to cut your own tree but you get a chance to do some alfresco weightlifting and get organic acupuncture.

At 8:00 a.m. on December 9—late in the cut-your-own tree season—we set out for a new farm a few miles from the old one. Only three cars had arrived ahead of us, which meant either that we'd found a hidden gem or that acres of Charlie Brown trees awaited. As we strolled, we found row after row of robust, well-shaped trees. They'd been grown a bit too close together, but that hadn't hampered their health or shapeliness as far as we could see. It didn't take us long to find good trees or farmhands to transport them back to the farmhouse. We pronounced the trip a resounding success, even after we got home and discovered that, as a result of growing so close together that inadequate space remained for pruning, each of our trees leans like a pine-scented Tower of Pisa.

2. Christmas Eve Mass: Too close to call. The Northern Virginia locals (my parents, my sister Lynne and her family, and I) go to Christmas Eve Mass at Nativity Parish in Burke every year. I never miss this ritual even though my agnostic status makes it a somewhat dicey proposition. I generally play it safe by staying silent during prayer recitations, avoiding communion, and following everyone else's lead.

This strategy was serving me well this year until we got to the "Sign of Peace," the part of the Mass where you shake hands with all the people around you. As the ritual Spreading of the Bacteria was coming to a close, I reached across my niece and nephew to shake hands with my brother-in-law. Unfortunately, my foot encountered the unexpected resistance of the kneeler and I lost my balance. Instead of placing my hand in my brother-in-law's, I came perilously close to reaching second base with my sister. I may have to rethink this tradition for next year. As should the hundreds of other lapsed Catholics who showed up and committed so many pre-Mass sins in the parking lot that the Church needed a pop-up confessional.

3. Christmas Eve with the Roommates: Jazz Hands. In 2011, I lived with Lynne, her husband, and their two kids (a.k.a "The Roommates") for nine months, which meant that I was in the house when the Roommates woke up on Christmas morning that year. They saw

this development as only slightly less miraculous than Santa's annual loot drop, and have asked me to spend the night at their house every Christmas Eve since. I'm grateful they still think their aunt is cool, so I'm always very happy to oblige. This year I arrived at my sister's house after Mass and found the Roommates in their pajamas, teeth brushed. By 9:00 p.m. they were tucked in, allowing Santa to get to work. He set up shop in the dining room, a bold move since both it and the living room (the place where the presents land) flank the stairs and are the first areas the kids would see if they made an unexpected appearance. I expressed this concern to my brother-in-law, but he felt certain the Roommates were down for the count. Half an hour into our work, which consisted of trying to piece together last year's wrapping paper scraps to achieve maximum box coverage (not because my sister is into sustainable wrapping but because she forgot to replenish her stock), I heard footsteps on the stairs and then saw my nephew on the landing.

"What are you doing?" he said.

Luckily, eleven years of practicing law had prepared me for just such a moment. Without hesitation I concocted a story that was seventy-five parts fact and twenty-five parts fiction (an unusually high truth ratio as alibis go, especially coming from a lawyer). I claimed that I forgot to lock the front door after making a trip out to my car for a bottle of champagne to share with the Roommates' parents, and that the three of us failed to hear Santa's entrance because we were busy boozing it up in the kitchen. I told this story from the middle of the full-size bed in my nephew's room, where I lay sandwiched between the two Roommates. I guess they decided to form an alliance once they realized they had a Situation on their hands.

When I finished, my niece said, "Will you stay with us, Aunt Wheat? I'm a little freaked out right now." Since I was partly to blame for this Santa credibility crisis, I couldn't refuse. And that's how yours truly, a woman who's great without child, ended up spending Christmas Eve with two kids. And in case you've ever wondered about the head-to-toe sleeping configuration? It only works in cartoons.

# 30

## A FISH OUT OF WATER

Just after Thanksgiving, I posted a profile on PlentyOfFish.com, an online dating site. I didn't expect many bites, given my timing. Starting a new relationship during the holidays can mean a trip across the gift expectations minefield. This dangerous terrain causes thousands of relationship casualties each year and an equally tragic number of Yankee Candle purchases.

I underestimated the willingness of men to throw themselves on the scented candle grenade, because correspondence flooded my in-box immediately. I suspected this had less to do with the appeal of my profile than the fact that I was just the most recent woman to fling herself into the sea. But I hoped my profile counted for something. I had put a fair amount of effort into it, mainly because I didn't want to waste my time or anyone else's. For example, because laughter matters so much to me, I didn't make a generic statement about having a good sense of humor; I gave specifics. To avoid getting paired up with someone who thinks *Dude, Where's My Car?* is the height of hilarity, I mentioned movies that I find funny, like *Airplane!* and *This Is Spinal Tap*.

Many men sent messages that picked up the movie thread and ran with it, to the point where if another man calls me "Shirley," you just might have to dust for vomit. (If these lines don't ring a bell, you should be watching those movies instead of reading this book.) Still, I responded to every single one of the movie quote guys because it was clear they'd at least read my profile. But for every "I picked the wrong day to stop sniffing glue" guy, there were at least as many whose entire message to me consisted of: "Hi." I was tempted to respond to this second group of men with the gentle suggestion that they upgrade to POF's Full Sentence Package ("Now featuring real commas!"). But I just sent those messages to the trash instead. Why bite on a hook that has no bait?

Some people may think my approach is unfair and that a two-character message is meant merely to create an opening. Maybe so, but to my eyes, those two characters were loaded with a completely different meaning. They said, "I'm not really trying, here." For all I know, the two-character, one-syllable guys sent the same message to every woman POF claimed might be a match, without even bothering to read her profile.

If I put this online interaction in real-world terms, it's kind of like a guy who walks into a crowded room and just waves randomly. Maybe he's waving at me, but I have no reason to assume so. Unless he comes over and says something that signals his interest in me specifically, I'm not about to curtail the conversation I'm having with the guy who asks me if I like David Sedaris. (Yes.) Am I judging too harshly? Missing out on good guys? Maybe. But to return to movies for a moment, this isn't *Jerry Maguire*, and you don't have me at "hello."

After communicating with a few men on POF, it was time to meet them in person.

The first three I met were nice, looked like the photos they posted or better, and showed no overt signs of insanity. One of them was even as funny as he claimed to be. Sounds great, right? It very well might have been, except that I felt absolutely nothing. I can't even explain it. As good as they looked on paper, these pairings were so flame retardant in real life they might as well have been wrapped in asbestos.

I had a fourth meet-up scheduled in the first week of January and found myself talking about it with my sister Lynne and my friend Philippa at Komi. Komi is one of D.C.'s Big Night Out restaurants, the kind of place where dinner takes four hours, features nine courses and wine pairings, and costs more than the rent in my first apartment.

Lynne and Philippa had been scheming to get to Komi for quite a while. It all started months earlier, when I had attracted the attention of a wealthy out-of-town suitor—a crush from my childhood, actually –who had a James Bond courting style. He would do things like ask me in passing where I was going to happy hour and then figure out how to have a bottle of wine sent to me there. The impressive precedent he set had Philippa and my sister convinced that, if I just happened to make casual mention of our Komi plans, he would immediately offer to treat us. He very well might have. He had followed the saga of Philippa's battle with breast cancer quite closely, knew that the post-surgery news was good, and probably would have enjoyed helping us celebrate that.

But just as we were finding out that Philippa was going to make it, I had realized the relationship wasn't.

Distance and too many other things were working against it. Lynne and Philippa, oblivious to the relationship's terminal diagnosis, jokingly kept up the pressure. "Komi, Komi, Komi," they chanted any time the three of us got together. I finally decided that I didn't need someone else to help me give them the celebration they wanted, I would do it myself. And it would cost me less than half a gum graft. I booked the reservation.

The three of us were halfway through our multi-course dinner when the topic of my imminent POF date came up. We had just washed down a savory course with a pour of Madeira. It was an odd pairing that somehow worked, creating a perfect segue into a discussion about dating.

I told Lynne and Philippa what I knew about the guy –good sense of humor based on his emails, attractive photos, family-oriented, employed —and Philippa said, "That description sounds promising enough, but *you* don't. You sound totally 'meh' about it." My sister nodded. I hated to admit it, but I knew they were right.

Much as I wanted a long-term relationship, my heart just wasn't into a fishing expedition. Maybe my lifelong aversion to shopping was the culprit. Cruising for men on a website felt a bit too much like scavenging the racks at TJ Maxx in search of the perfect little black dress. Maybe a shift in priorities was to blame. I had chosen to dedicate more of my free time on creative pursuits, like writing and podcasting, which left me little time for dating. Or maybe, as Philippa speculated, I just hadn't met the right person.

Whatever the reason, my love life was starting to seem like Charlie Brown's football, and I was tired of making unsuccessful attempts to kick it. But I'm not giving up on the game; I'm just taking a timeout. I will try again, and one of these days I'll connect. I just know it.

# 31

## A DAY TO REMEMBER

A year ago today, my grandmother passed away. It also happened to be the day when my dear friend, Joseph, turned 40. Joseph is what people refer to as a character or, as he sometimes puts it, "an acquired taste." I can vouch for the fact that not everyone knows how to take Joseph's bawdy sense of humor, which isn't weighed down by concerns about propriety or other people's comfort. Taking this into account, my 100% Italian, 100% Catholic, utterly proper grandmother should have been the last person on earth to develop a soft spot for Joseph. Yet Nana loved him. I never asked her why, but I think I can guess.

It wasn't the simple fact that, because Joseph had been my sidekick since 1995, he tended to show up at family events. Nor was it because he did things like ask her to dance with him at my cousin's wedding. (This gesture was nowhere near as gallant as it sounds. Dancing with Joseph is like being a rock tied to the end of a catapult. At some point, centrifugal force will forcibly eject you and send you flying, resulting in mass casualties wherever you land.) Nor was it the fact that, when my grandmother was living with my parents in 2008, Joseph would drop by to have lunch and play Yahtzee with her. Like the dancing, this wasn't as cute as it sounds, either. Those two were to Yahtzee what Rocky Balboa and Apollo Creed were to boxing. Somehow my grandmother always maintained a slight edge.

Joseph's explanation? "Nana cheats."

Yahtzee shark or not, my grandmother adored Joseph, and I chalk it up to one simple reason: she could tell how much he loved me and my family. When Nana died on Joseph's birthday, I joked with my family that she'd done it on purpose so she could have the last laugh. But in reality, if she did it on purpose, it was in tribute. The minute my sister Suzi relayed the news that Nana had passed away, I wanted to tell Joseph what happened, to get his support as I grieved. But I couldn't reach him.

I understood very well that friendships age the same way people do: inevitably, but not predictably.

Some grow old with grace and dignity, others with neither. The years had mainly been kind to my friendship with Joseph, right up until I married the Lawnmower in 2010. Male/female friendships often take it on the chin when a truly significant other enters the picture, especially when the friend and the S.O. have opposite personalities, as the LM and Joseph did.

Joseph is the kind of guy who took one look at the tree house behind my old house and said, "We've got to host a redneck picnic there." (The picnic spread, which consisted of Spam, Cheez-Whiz, and Franzia, gave me one of the worst hangovers I've ever had.) My ex-husband, by contrast, had probably renounced both tree houses and Cheez-Whiz by age seven.

Everything had gone well enough between Joseph and the LM at first. In fact, my then-fiancé even asked Joseph to be a groomsmen in our wedding. But less than two months into our marriage, my husband declared Joseph unwelcome in his household based on a perceived insult. (I soon learned the man I married was an expert insult perceiver.)

I maintained my friendship with Joseph but it was strained. He couldn't show up at family gatherings anymore, and that hurt. We still got together regularly, which I never hid from my husband, but we weren't the same. I felt uncomfortable talking about anything involving my marriage, making a huge chunk of my life conversationally off-limits. The friendship, while technically alive, fell into a persistent vegetative state.

It gained a new lease on life in the summer of 2011, when I left the LM. To Joseph's everlasting credit, he never said, "I told you so" or blamed me for the near-death of our friendship. He offered me his full support, no questions asked. We got back into the habit of spending time together every week and he opened up his home to me. I would go over there most Tuesday nights to make dinner –a simple pleasure I missed while my life was in flux—and vent while he listened and poured wine. Joseph helped me through that time in ways I will never forget.

Less than a year later, as I was settling into my post-divorce life, Joseph Met Someone. When he told me about it, I was excited because no one deserved relationship happiness more than him (except for me, of course). I expected our friendship to change if his new relationship progressed, but I hoped we'd find a way to stay close. And I vowed to accept whatever changes came gracefully, just as Joseph had.

Well, we didn't manage to find a way to stay close, and my vow went right out the window the day Nana died. I couldn't reach Joseph because he was in Puerto Rico, celebrating his 40th birthday with the girlfriend who had moved in with him. I understood intellectually that this was an excellent reason for his absence and that I should feel happy for him. Instead, I felt lousy—as if I'd lost my grandmother and my best friend on the same day.

A year later, I've adjusted to Nana being gone and to the change in my and Joseph's friendship. (He's married now.) I'm grateful for the incredible memories those two gave me, but I'd be lying if I said I didn't miss them both, terribly.

# 32

## EASY AS PI(E)

My mother went out of town for a few days last Saturday, leaving my father home alone. This state of affairs always makes me a little uneasy. Dad's perfectly capable of taking care of himself, but he's not exactly gifted when it comes to domestic stuff. He occasionally mistakes the washer for the dryer, and his cooking repertoire consists of dishes whose names involve words like "Oodles" and "Umm." To make sure Dad wouldn't subsist entirely on a diet of fried baloney, I invited him to join me at two food-centric events I'd been invited to last weekend: a pi(e) party on Saturday evening and a book-signing party on Sunday afternoon.

The pi(e) party is a festive annual bash my friends host to celebrate the number 3.14, one of the few things

I remember from years of math classes. They always schedule it as close to March 14 as possible and fete the famous number by putting out a massive assortment of sweet and savory pies. No one in his right mind turns down a legitimate chance to scarf up a bunch of pie and call it "dinner," so I knew Dad was a shoo-in for that event.

I felt less certain he'd want to go to the book party. According to the invitation my friend Sue had sent, Peter Baker, a best-selling author of political nonfiction, would talk about his latest work while guests enjoyed drinks and hors d'oeuvres. Dad likes news but finds much of politics distasteful. Would the prospect of a best-selling author and cocktail meatballs whet Dad's appetite enough to stomach a bit of politics?

He said, "Why not? It sounds interesting," which I knew meant, "They'll have Vienna sausages, right?"

Dad and I got to the pi(e) party fairly early last Saturday evening because years of attending had taught me to show up in the first wave of eaters. We loaded up our plates with goodies and parked ourselves on a couch a few feet away from the swelling crowd.

As we started in on our samplers, Dad turned to me and said, "I know you think I don't listen to you, Wheat, but sometimes I actually do." I couldn't wait for

Dad to go on. Rarely does an adult child get to experience the gratification of hearing she knows something her father doesn't.

He raised a forkful of coconut crème pie and announced, "I want to die at home."

My father sure knows how to liven up a party.

Hearing that gem from Dad made me wish I'd kept my pie hole shut months earlier instead of droning on about long-term care planning. I also began to wonder whether inviting him to the book bash was such a great idea.

The next day, Dad and I met at my place at four o'clock, and I drove us over to Sue's home in McLean, a nearby suburb. Sue and her husband live in a lovely, tree-lined neighborhood where stately brick homes are separated from each other by a respectful, but not unfriendly, distance. The hostess herself greeted us at the door, welcomed Dad with the warmth of a lifelong friend, and told us to make ourselves at home.

We went straight to the dining room and the refreshments. I scooped stuffed grape leaves and olives onto a small plate as I admired the unpretentious elegance of the dining room. Another guest struck up a conversation with me. She introduced herself and said she'd come to the party with her husband. She pointed at him, and I saw that he was chatting with Dad. I felt a pang of anxiety. What if Dad decided to spring his new "Die in Place" policy on this unsuspecting guest? I was thinking only of that as I took my plastic fork and stabbed the lone olive on my plate. Or tried to.

Instead of pinning the hors d'oeuvre, my fork got only the faintest hold on it, a hold that it surrendered abruptly. The liberated olive sailed across the dining room, landed on the floor, and rolled like a marble until it came to rest inches from Sue's right toe. She didn't seem to notice, and I thought I might get away with my faux pas until I caught my father's eye across the room and saw him smirking. The book talk soon got underway, and the author proved to be a witty, engaging, funny speaker. Dad looked like he was enjoying himself and I relaxed.

The talk ended and I offered to retrieve our coats from a room on the opposite side of the house. When I returned to the dining room with coats in hand, Dad had vanished. I didn't see him as I worked my way through the crowded kitchen and family room. I headed toward the front door—still no sign of him. As I stood in the foyer trying to figure out where he might have gone, I heard a loud noise coming from my immediate left. There, a closed door was being rattled in its frame by an unseen and panicked force.

*Oh no, Dad's locked himself in the bathroom!* Compared to this, the flying olive was nothing.

I grabbed the doorknob and gave it a hard yank. The door flew open and out came not my father but a very exuberant spaniel, which shot into the crowded living room like a fur missile. Just then, my father appeared beside me. I didn't have to ask if he'd seen the whole thing, because he was once again tittering. We made a hasty exit.

I can't claim that this story has a moral, but I did learn two things: Dad isn't the one you can't take anywhere, I am. And sometimes "Who let the dogs out?" is not a rhetorical question.

# 33

## DOING THE MATH

From time to time, I pick up my elementary school-aged niece and nephew, aka the Roommates, at their bus stop and hang out with them until their parents get home. I love doing the after-school shift.

Sometimes it involves helping the kids with their homework, which I don't mind at all, but there are some subjects I enjoy more than others. My taste skews heavily toward the language arts, just as it did when I was in elementary school. I will happily quiz the Roommates all day on spelling and vocabulary, and I'm delighted to help them with their writing. But that excitement morphs into something closer to dread when they bring me a piece of math.

Though I had a knack for math, I hated it as a kid, and I still do. The subject matter doesn't intimidate me, and I'm not worried that the kids' math knowledge has surpassed mine (though we've got to be getting close); math just bores me. And to make matters worse, some genius up and changed the terminology, which I discovered while helping my nephew with the following subtraction problem:

425

−298
———

My nephew recognized that he had an issue right off the bat because 5 is smaller than 8. Back in my elementary school days, if the "ones" suddenly found themselves in this situation, where they were just a little short, they'd go right next door and hit up the "tens" for a loan. Our term for this was "borrowing."

Maybe it was a bit of a misnomer because the ones, like parasitic family members, had absolutely no intention of paying the tens back. But for all of its shortcomings, "borrowing" beats the pants off of the new math slang. The current word for this transaction, my nephew informed me, is "regrouping."

This term may be new, but I'm not so sure it's improved, and I wonder where in the world it came from. It reeks faintly of pop psychology, as if the ones just lost their way and need a group hug from the tens to set them straight. Or maybe the Great Recession is to blame. Perhaps debt has become so un-chic that we can't come right out and call it what it is. Instead, we euphemize it wherever we find it, even in the elementary math sector. (God forbid we risk hurting the ones' fragile self-esteem.)

Whatever the reason for eliminating "borrowing" from the math lexicon, I don't like it. And surely we can find a better term for it than "regrouping," because that's what I call it when I'm doing subtraction in my love life, not on a chalkboard.

# 34

## FAMILY VACATIONS, THEY'RE A REAL TRIP

Family vacations were a big deal when I was growing up. Mom and Dad hadn't taken trips like that when they were kids, so they wanted to make sure my siblings and I got to experience something they didn't: a chance to take our fighting on the road. Aside from giving us new scenery for our bickering, our family vacations also created enduring memories. This became a topic of conversation at the office yesterday as my friend Don was telling me about his family's plans for spring break.

Knowing that Don and his wife have taken their kids, now eleven and seventeen, to places like Lake Tahoe, Barcelona, and Tuscany, I asked, "Are you guys headed someplace cool again this year?"

"We'd planned to," Don said, "but by the time we decided to book a trip, a lot of our top choices were out of the question. So now we're going to…Fort Lauderdale." He said this as if Fort Lauderdale were the travel equivalent of walking the Green Mile.

"What's wrong with that? I mean, spring break at the beach doesn't exactly suck." He laughed.

"Yeah, that's what I thought until my son said, 'If we're not going out of the country, I'm not goin'.'"

Had I tried that on my parents when I was that age, Dad would have said, "Don't worry, kid, I'm about to kick your ass to Mexico."

I offered to give Don's son a call and a dose of perspective by telling him all about the vacation my family took when I was five to Ferrum College in, where else, Ferrum, Virginia. Ferrum College, "The Harvard of Roanoke," is located in the foothills of the Blue Ridge Mountains in the southwestern part of the commonwealth. I don't know how my parents came to choose this particular vacation destination. Maybe all the prisons in Virginia were booked that week.

From what I remember of our stay in Ferrum, we slept in fifty-thread-count luxury in dorm rooms, ate gourmet dining hall fare like turkey tetrazzini, and spent our days digging ditches. I'm kidding about that last part. I think. I distinctly recall spending our days doing all sorts of fun outdoors activities like horseback riding.

Our last outdoorsy activity of the week was a tubing excursion on the Roanoke River. Since a trip to the grocery store with the four of us kids qualified as high adventure, you have to wonder what my parents were thinking. I'm sure they also wondered what they'd been thinking once our guide informed us that we would have to wear our clothes over our bathing suits the whole time. We hopped in our tubes and set off, because nothing screams "family fun" like floating down a river in waterlogged jeans.

Speaking of screaming, my brother, L.J., did not seem overly enamored with our tubing adventure. He wailed non-stop, perhaps because at three years of age he had only recently exited the whole soggy drawers business. To bring the situation under control, my parents divided and conquered along gender lines. Mom looped her limbs through my and my sisters' tubes, and our four-person formation began to bob along peacefully.

Or it would have, if my sister Suzi hadn't pointed to an object floating beside her and said, "That's a snake, Mom!"

Our mother took one look and said, "No, that's a stick," making her the first person ever to see a floating tree limb with eyeballs.

We might have celebrated this important botanical discovery had we not been distracted by the ongoing shenanigans in the boy faction. My brother's screaming was relentless. Yet even over the din, Dad, who has always been afraid of snakes, must have heard Suzi's pronouncement. He grabbed my brother and the tubes and hopped ashore. Dad soon learned that he and L.J. weren't the only ones who'd decided to make a break for dry land. Just to my father's right, a nest of snakes had clustered on the shore to bask in the glow of the Ferrum sun. As I told Don, the ensuing screams still hang in the heavens to this day.

"Here's my son's number," he said.

# 35

## LETTING IT ALL HANG OUT

Two weekends ago, my father, at 71 years of age, suddenly found himself face-to-face with a bunch of singing, naked people. No, he had not joined the chorus at a nudist colony; he'd gone with me and my mother to see "Hair" at the Keegan Theater in D.C., and we were sitting in the second row.

Nothing in my life had prepared me for that particular moment, and I'm fairly certain Dad didn't see it coming, either. For openers, Dad is not a culture guy. He loves sports, and his idea of high art is watching Roy Halladay pitch a perfect game for the Phillies. He appreciates a good play or musical from time to time, but he doesn't go out of his way for it. In fact, it usually takes some convincing to get him to trade nine innings for two acts. It was particularly impressive, then, that Mom got him to agree to see "Hair," because the very name of the show refers to something Dad hasn't had on his head in years.

I wasn't around to hear Mom's sales pitch, but I bet she chose not to burden my father with the nitty-gritty of the plot. She probably told him it was a musical about the '60s and left it at that. Mom would have known that, had she offered a more complete description of the show —a bunch of hippies singing about sex, drugs and war in graphic detail —my straight-laced father might not have left the house. Or maybe she just wanted Dad to be surprised. I could relate to that. I wanted to be surprised, too. Going into the show, I purposely avoided reading reviews, synopses, or any other press.

On the night of the show, our group, which included two of my aunts and uncles and a few of their friends, arrived at the Keegan at 7:45. The theater is a beautiful, all-brick building near Dupont Circle, an affluent neighborhood in the northwest quadrant of D.C. Built in 1905, the Keegan originally served as the gymnasium for a girls school. Since its conversion to a performing arts venue, the Keegan has shed its gym image but not so much the 1905 part. Nowhere is this more evident than in its two restrooms. Located in the basement, each is a "one-holer" that features what I suspected was original plumbing, as well as a sign above the toilet that reads: Please jiggle the handle.

My father must have felt right at home on seeing this public endorsement of his solution to every plumbing problem. But any goodwill he was feeling shot right out the window when, during the first minute of the play, one of the male leads performed an extended pantomime of self-gratification.

As I sat next to my father, I was truly beside myself. I thought I might escape via spontaneous combustion, based on the amount of heat that had sprung to my cheeks. When that didn't work, I did what any mature, professional 42 year-old woman would do: I snickered uncontrollably. Dad's face, by contrast, looked like something out of Easter Island. We somehow made it all the way through the first act, despite one song whose title and lyrics sounded like entries in *Roget's Thesaurus: Human Mating Edition.*

During the intermission, my parents and I chatted with my relatives, pointedly omitting mention of the unsavory stuff and instead praising the cast for its vocal skills, costumes, and willingness to abandon all grooming habits in order to get in character. We returned to our seats and everything was going fine until the middle of Act Two, when the Hippies decided to stage a "be-in" at a park.

I was born in 1971 and had no idea what a "be-in" was. I learned it's short for "be in your birthday suit" as the ensemble burst into song and out of their clothes. They sang as a full Monty chorus line for a minute that felt like a year. Forget "Let the Sunshine In"; the moons had taken center stage. I couldn't bear to look at my father. The show ended shortly after that—a mercy killing—and the cast began to take its bows. Dad, who hadn't applauded a single time during the show, stunned me by being one of the first people to leap to his feet and clap with genuine enthusiasm.

When I asked him about it afterwards, he said, "The music wasn't exactly my cup of tea, and the whole thing's a little dated, but they gave it everything they had, and they were great." He was absolutely right, because the production was nothing short of top-notch.

I had underestimated my father, as I've done many times over the course of my life. I should have known that, instead of dwelling on the stuff he didn't like, my father would look past form, focus on substance, and zero in on the naked truth.

# 36

## THE LOCH NESS MAN-STERS

I spent Sunday afternoon on the loveseat in my living room, alternating between writing and staring out the back window. (Only a trained eye can tell the difference between these two activities.) During one of the staring periods, my eyes swore they caught sight of two men clad in jeans and polo shirts, rising up out of my ivy-covered backyard like a pair of preppy Loch Ness Monsters.

When your eyes report something like this, your brain is supposed to step in and supply a plausible explanation. My brain was not up to the task. When pressed to explain how these guys got into my fenced-in backyard and what they were doing there, it assured me they were Arlington County employees. Doing a weekend kudzu census, one assumes.

In the face of such a flimsy theory, I had no choice but to go outside and investigate. It didn't occur to me to arm myself because at that moment I wasn't thinking self-defense, I was thinking: blog content. I marched out the side door and was standing in the backyard before I realized I had no idea what I was supposed to say.

"Hi," I said, trying to sound like an authoritative property owner. Or as authoritative as a property owner can sound while wearing yoga pants and a pink hoodie. The intruders looked sheepish, uncomfortable, and definitely younger than thirty. One was quite tall and the other not at all, leading me to mentally dub them Mutt and Jeff.

"Hey," Mutt and Jeff said in unison. Since they didn't call me "ma'am," I decided they had come in peace. But I still didn't know why, so I asked. Their answer made me feel like I was reading The Onion's police blotter. Mutt explained that, earlier in the day, he and Jeff decided to take advantage of the gorgeous spring weather with a walk on Arlington's Four Mile Run Trail. Somewhere along the way, the trail goes beneath an overpass, and at that point the men spotted a large, tunnel-like opening.

"You know, a culvert," said Jeff, French-ifying it so that it came out as "cul-vare." Mutt shook his head.

"Dude, it's culvert," he said, giving the ending a hard "t." He probably understood that there's only so much you can do to class up a sewer.

"Are you sure?" Jeff said. "I mean, I always thought it was cul-vare." I fought the urge to smack my forehead.

"Cul-vare, cul-vert, tomay-to, tomah-to," I said. "What happened when you got to the thing?"

Mutt and Jeff were curious, as most people would be. As only twenty-something male people would do, they went in. The two wandered through the tunnel without incident at first. But eventually the tunnel narrowed, forcing them to walk in a less than vertical position and to have very close encounters with spiders of every kind.

"And how long did you guys go like that?" I asked.

"Oh, about an hour and a half," said Mutt, proving that, even in a tunnel, men would rather tussle with mutant spiders than turn around or, God forbid, ask one of the spiders for directions.

Just as the conditions were getting too uncomfortable to bear, the two men spotted a rope of some sort suspended from the top of the tunnel. Confident that it was linked to a possible way out, they followed it. Sure enough, that rope was attached to a metal lid that, unbeknownst to me, was a portal into my ivy. I couldn't help but feel a bit sorry for the duo, standing there covered in dirt and who knows what else, so I offered them a beer and invited them to have a seat at the table on my patio.

They accepted without hesitation. As the three of us sat in the sun, sipped cold beer and made small talk, Jeff asked me what type of work I did. I found it a reassuring consistency to know that, no matter where or how you meet a man in D.C., he's guaranteed to ask you what you do for a living. I threw the question ball back and learned that Jeff was a teacher. I think we can all sleep a little easier knowing that the leaders of tomorrow are being groomed by someone who wanders off of a perfectly good trail in favor of spelunking in a sewer.

If nothing else, this episode proves that the people who tell me I'll meet a man when I least expect it are right. But the men don't come crawling out of the woodwork; they come out of the ivy.

# 37

## KILL THE WABBIT

Last year I volunteered to don a rabbit suit for my neighborhood's annual Easter celebration. I faced some major costume adversity along the way, but it was nothing that a seasoned mascot professional like me couldn't handle. Impressed by my rookie outing, my neighbor Toni asked me to suit up again this year. This time she gave me more notice—skills like mine are in high demand—and that allowed me to negotiate new terms of engagement.

First, I requested a transportation upgrade. Last year I walked to the venue and used the nearby home of two complete strangers as my dressing room. This made for a rather awkward moment when I had to ask one of them to glue my eye back onto my face. I also insisted that the costume be brought up to code. The mascot industry might overlook a single year as a one-eyed rabbit, but two in a row could easily relegate me to low-paying niche roles. Toni agreed to have the costumed repaired and to drop it off the night before so I could change in the comfort of my own home. She also committed to have an escort pick me up and bring me to the park. I wasn't home when Toni dropped off the newly repaired costume last night, but she sent me a message to let me know she'd left it for me.

"No blog entries about random animal carcasses being left on your doorstep," she texted.

Writing that sort of a post was the last thing on my mind when I pulled the costume out of the bag, largely because "random animal carcass" would have been paying it a major compliment. The wayward right eye had been meticulously reapplied, which helped, but it concerned me to see that a paperclip had been deployed to keep a neck seam together. And then there was the matter of the face. Even with both eyes intact, it didn't evoke Bugs Bunny so much as Munch's "The Scream."

I stepped into the suit at 9:50 a.m. and confirmed that it was still the same oxygen and sensory deprivation chamber I remembered. At 9:55, a late-model Volvo sedan pulled into the driveway. (I know these details only because my housemate relayed them to me.)

The driver and a handler emerged and escorted me to the car, and we rode to the park in what I assume was climate-controlled comfort.

As soon as I got out of the car, Toni announced my presence on a megaphone and kicked off the hunt. To ensure that the older kids didn't overrun the little ones, the organizers staged the hunt in different sections of the park according to age. Since my target audience was kids under five, I wandered off toward what looked like the shortest group of blobs. My instincts were correct and led me to the youngest kids.

Their hunt, however, had been infiltrated by one slightly older and precocious child who said, "Wait a minute, that's a person. I see human skin."

I'm sure he did. The bunny suit paws were not attached to the body, so my skin was exposed any time I attempted movement more strenuous than a shrug. The smallest children didn't seem to notice, but this kid's parents probably had to come up with some sort of an explanation. Maybe they told him the Easter bunny had a touch of mange.

This year, just like last year, lots of little kids wanted to hug me. (And my stalker was back, though she didn't seem quite as excited to see me. I think she's moved on to Santa Claus.) But for every child that

loved me, there was at least one more who fled screaming, as if he had not been visited by the Easter bunny
but sprayed by the Easter skunk.

A less confident mascot might be dismayed by a
bad hug-to-scream ratio, but I know it's no reflection
on my skills. I firmly believe they'll want me back next
year, and I intend to make a few more demands when
I renegotiate my contract. In addition to valet service,
I expect one more handler, because a mascot of my
caliber warrants an entourage. Not to mention a costume change. It's about time to pull a new rabbit out
of the hat.

# 38

## SURRENDER AT YORKTOWN

Field trips sure have changed since I was a student at Orange Hunt Elementary School in the late '70s and early '80s. I discovered this yesterday, when I went with my nephew Timothy's fourth-grade class to Jamestown and Yorktown.

Students of Revolutionary War history know that these two towns played crucial roles not just in Virginia's history but also in the struggle for American independence. I played a far less significant role on Timothy's trip. I don't know quite how to describe what I did, but I'm certain I wasn't a chaperone. My non-chaperone status came about because the bus had only so many extra seats, many adults had volunteered to go, and my name had not been picked when the teacher held a drawing. Losing this lottery made me as sad as not getting selected for audit by the IRS. Fresh cause for despair arrived days before the trip when my nephew informed me that he really wanted me to go and that I still could if I just drove myself. My boss, an otherwise wonderful person, cleared the last obstacle to my attendance by refusing to claim that he needed me at work that day.

I gave in and agreed to go because, when it comes right down to it, I love being a Rent-A-'Rent to my niece and nephews. I had mixed feelings about not riding with the kids, however. On the one hand, I would get 320 miles' worth of fourth-grader-free peace and quiet. On the other, the window of time available to embarrass my nephew had just shrunk dramatically, and I could no longer justify bringing a flask on the trip.

I arrived at the school at 6:45 a.m. on the day of the field trip and found several other parents who also intended to drive. Various individual constraints made carpooling impossible, so we decided just to follow the buses, like a bunch of environmentally irresponsible groupies.

Speaking of the buses, these were not the regulation yellow Fairfax County buses that took me on field trips as a kid. They were proper motor coaches, the kind you'd expect to ride to Atlantic City in your sunset years to play nickel slots and see Wayne Newton perform (posthumously) at the Golden Nugget. These buses had bathrooms, air conditioning, and a DVD player. When I was a kid, climate control on the bus entailed lowering your window—if you had the strength to squeeze together the ancient metal latches at the top that held it in place. There were no bathrooms, and onboard entertainment consisted of singing "99 Bottles of Beer On The Wall." (I'm pretty sure we picked that up from our chaperones.) Timothy's class was very excited about getting to watch *Frozen* on the trip but disappointed to learn that the in-bus bathroom was to be used "only for emergencies."

"You mean we can't go in and look around?" one kid asked, as if he'd been deprived of a chance to see the Taj Mahal rather than a rolling Port-A-Potty.

The caravan set off and arrived in Jamestown a little more than three hours later. Because my car has no in-cabin restroom, I had an urgent need to find the facilities. (My desire to embarrass my nephew did not include the willingness to go down in grade school folklore as the aunt who wet her pants.) I also had to buy a ticket, because groupies handle their own logistics.

Jamestown was absolutely teeming with grade schoolers, so I made sure I knew where Timothy's class had congregated before I went to run my two little errands. I wasn't too worried about time, nor did it occur to me to find out what the class plans were, because I figured a horde of fourth graders couldn't move any faster than fingernails grow.

I misfigured. I returned to the spot to find that Timothy's class had departed. To make matters worse, no bystanders knew where they'd gone. A staff member told me the class might be at one of three sites—the "Indian village," the colonial settlement, or the ship replicas—or anywhere in between. I'd been at Jamestown for all of ten minutes and somehow had managed to lose my nephew already. I almost felt proud of myself, knowing it would take your average sitcom character at least fifteen minutes to pull off a mishap like that.

I contemplated my options. I could join up with the group of parents and students standing a few feet away from me. They seemed nice. But then my thoughts returned to my nephew, to whom I'd like to leave a legacy that consists of something more than abandonment issues. I strode off, armed with a strong sense of purpose and a weak sense of direction.

A few moments later, I spotted oval-shaped wigwams and a profoundly potbellied man who was naked but for two fur flaps that hung at his waist like cocktail napkins on a clothesline. I'd landed at the Indian village or Myrtle Beach. I didn't spot Timothy's class there, so I followed a path to the next site: the settlement. I was canvassing the area in search of my lost nephew when a musket fired directly behind me, nearly causing me to lose control of my bowels.

I beat a hasty retreat and was making my way to the ships when I heard a familiar voice yell, "Aunt Wheat! Where did you GO?" I acted nonchalant and blamed it on the logistical burdens we non-chaperones are forced to bear.

After that, things went more smoothly. Timothy's class behaved well and mainly paid attention to the tour guides. In fact, a bunch of the kids raised their hands to answer when the guide stood in front of the replica of a house and asked, "Does anyone know what wattle and daub is?"

"A colonial law firm," I said before I could stop myself. My nephew groaned and put a hand over his eyes. Several other kids gave me strange looks and then some smarty-pants started nattering on about a primitive construction process. As luck would have it, the guide had timed our arrival in the settlement area to coincide with the musket demonstration. I was able to enjoy it the second time, freed from the fear that I was being shot at by a colonial sniper.

After lunch we made the short trip to Yorktown. Fatigue was beginning to set in, but the kids were all ears when our guide started to talk about herbs and medicines used by the colonists. She held up a stalk of dried tobacco and told the kids its purpose was "upward and downward purging." She explained that eating a small amount of dried tobacco would have caused the patient to throw up. Believing that she'd given the kids the kind of hint that would encourage deductive reasoning, she then asked them how the colonists might have used the tobacco for a "downward purge." Hands shot up, and she called on a kid at random.

"They stuck it up their butts?" he ventured. Even the guide couldn't keep an entirely straight face.

After that, the kids watched a cooking demonstration, scraped at a drying animal hide, crawled around inside an infantry tent, and witnessed yet another musket demo. Finally it was time for the attraction they'd all been waiting for: the gift shop. I supervised the shopping trip, an experience that convinced me the patriots' Revolutionary War arsenal should have included a very small gift shop packed with rambunctious fourth graders. Ten minutes in there would have brought the whole British Empire to its knees.

The gift shop was the final item on the agenda. Despite being a mere groupie, I was given permission to drive Timothy home, and we left Yorktown just before 5:00 p.m. Torrential rain slowed us down for long stretches, so I didn't get back to my own house until 8:30 p.m. I was in my pajamas and ready for bed by 8:31, proving that at least one aspect of field trips has stayed exactly the same.

# 39

## LET US PRAY, AND
## HEAVEN HELP US

I used to say my law degree was my greatest professional achievement. Not anymore, folks. The ol' Juris Doctor lost its exalted status today, when I became a woman of the cloth.

No, I did not join a convent (though after my ruinous marriage, it's not that far-fetched a scenario). I got ordained as a minister in the Universal Life Church so I could perform the wedding of my dear friends Michelle and Ken. The ULC's motto is "We are all children of the same universe," because "pay us and we'll make you a minister" sounded too tacky. I joke, but the ULC has standards. It's not one of those faux churches that thinks nothing of ordaining, for example, a housecat. To become a ULC minister, you must at the very least have opposable thumbs and a Visa.

Michelle and Ken didn't expect to ask me to marry them any more than I expected to be asked. Their wedding had been scheduled for months and they had our friend Tim all lined up, ordained and ready to preside. Unfortunately, Tim got called away for a family emergency, and Ken and Michelle hadn't thought to designate an understudy.

I was a natural choice to fill in due to my vast wedding experience. I've been in sixteen weddings and played all sorts of different roles (seventeen if you count the one where I was a bride.) I've served as a bridesmaid, played the piano and organ, read biblical passages, and juggled fire. Of course, the fire juggling wasn't so much an official duty as the natural consequence of being unwilling to let go of my drink when the sleeve of my polyester bridesmaid dress got too close to a lit candle.

I jumped at the chance to officiate for my friends. With Michelle and Ken's wedding only five days away, I had to act fast. I submitted my application to the ULC at 4:23 p.m. and held my breath. After an agonizing deliberative process that lasted a nanosecond, a committee comprised of zeroes and ones informed me that I was official. To expedite the arrival of my credentials,

I bought the "Emergency Minister's Package," an offering whose unfortunate name makes it sound like a set of spare clergy privates. Had I not been pressed for time, I might have continued shopping at the ULC Minister Store, which sells, among other things, "Doctor of Metaphysics" certificates and the always-popular "Ministry-in-a-Box."

Anyway, I'm official. As a result of my new status, I am also now qualified to perform baptisms, and funerals, and I can even start my own congregation. So from here on out, please feel free to call me "Irreverend," and yes, I do take American Express.

# 40

## HOW HARD CAN IT BE?

**M**y friend Larry and I had planned to meet for a drink at a neighborhood pizza joint last night. I texted to let him know I might be a few minutes late because I needed to stop by the variety store near the restaurant to pick up some duct tape. Very few places can legitimately call themselves variety stores these days, but this place earns the name. One half of the store features nails, screwdrivers and home maintenance necessities, while the other half has toasters, wagons, and other garage sale inventory. We locals love the place. And we don't mind paying a little extra to skip a trip to Home Depot and take a nostalgia trip in return. I knew the store would have the duct tape I needed.

I also knew my friend would both accept my tardiness and want to know nothing whatsoever about why I needed duct tape. (Maybe that explains why he and I get along so well.) Though Larry didn't ask, I needed it for what I thought was a good reason: plumbing.

My friend Wayne, a carpenter and all-around handyman, heard about this later and said, "Of course. Because all good plumbing jobs start off with duct tape." What Wayne didn't know was that I had never tried to start any kind of plumbing job before, much less a good one. I had always called in the pros because I respect the plumbing in my house. When I realized after two years that the feeling wasn't mutual, I decided to try to increase my esteem in the eyes of the pipes by taking on what seemed like an entry-level problem: a slow draining tub.

I got out the Google, landed on a DIY plumbing forum, and got more suggestions than I really ever wanted or needed. Fortunately, some of them seemed like things I had a shot at pulling off, especially if I could force myself to ignore something else Wayne once said: "Five words always get me in trouble: How hard can it be?"

The first DIY suggestion that made any sense came from the old school and has become popular again thanks to the "green" contingent: Flush the drain with a mixture of baking soda and vinegar. I remembered using the same combination to make faux volcanoes when I was a kid and could not resist a chance to recreate Vesuvius in my tub. Alas, the experiment was nowhere near as effective as it was fun.

I went back to the drawing board and read about clearing drain blockages with a plunger, a device that was somehow absent from my arsenal of household necessities. (But I do have three pie slicers and two cake knives, so if a major pastry emergency breaks out, as they are wont to do, I'm ready.) To close the gap in my inventory, I stopped by Home Depot after work one day and arrived at the plumbing aisle with every intention of buying only a plunger.

I was trying to figure out which plunger to select from no fewer than 17 varieties when a vision of plumbing seduction got my attention. Sitting on a shelf right in front of me was a product that not only won a "Consumer's Choice" award but looked like something Wile E. Coyote would own. It had compressed gas canisters and the kind of hand pump you'd use to detonate dynamite. It cost $24.88. Some people might think that's a high price to pay for a classed-up plunger, but if you can resist that purchase, you're not human. I also bought a simple bellows plunger, just in case.

I got home and my excitement to try out the new gizmo evaporated as soon as I realized I couldn't use it without first sealing off the overflow valve on the tub. This required duct tape, something else that I lacked. And that's how I ended up at the local variety store. I made my purchase and met my friend.

After a fun-filled evening and three beers, I walked home. I was ready to deploy the fancy plunger, because everyone knows there's no better time to do a little DIY plumbing than after consuming three beers. Knowing that I'd had a few, I decided that if I managed to open the package without incident, it would prove I was competent enough to use the device. (Mensa gives its applicants a similar IQ test.)

The package opening was uneventful, despite the fact that it involved scissors, so I plowed ahead, casting a glance in the general direction of the instructions. I absorbed portions of the diagram by telepathy and determined I was ready to load and lock. The contraption consisted of three parts –a suction cup base, a long plastic tube, and a T-shaped pump handle topped by a yellow plastic knob—that looked like they were meant to be screwed together eventually. The long plastic tube happened to be the widest piece of the three and seemed a natural place to drop in the gas canister, so I did that first. It took some effort to shove it in there, but I managed. I then screwed the rest of the apparatus together, duct-taped the overflow valve, let the tub fill, and prepared to work my magic.

I positioned the suction cup base on top of the drain and knelt on the floor so I would have maximum leverage while operating the plunger. I pushed down on the T-shaped handles with all of my might. I failed to achieve traction with the suction cup, causing it to slip off of the bottom of the tub and shoot to the side, and causing me to topple over and get doused with displaced water as I fell. I made another attempt. The second time, I took care in placing the suction cup over the drain to make sure it adhered. It felt right. I leaned on the handle to detonate the device and awaited a satisfying blast of compressed air. Nothing happened. No resistance, no "pffft," no nothing.

After trying one more time, I went back to the instructions, whereupon I learned that the gas canisters don't go in the long, plastic tube but rather inside the little yellow knob on top of the pump. Duh, everyone knows that, right? Well, maybe the people that actually read the directions do. I thought I could rectify my goof simply by dumping out the cartridge I had loaded. When I unscrewed the tube and turned it upside-down, I discovered the cartridge was just a touch wider than the tube opening, an issue that could be overcome with a big, forceful blast of air but not with gravity. I left the cartridge rattling around in the tube like a BB in a bass drum. Not wanting to waste my MacGyver duct-tape job, I decided to go ahead and try the bellows plunger. It worked perfectly on the very first try, of course. Despite the fact that the most effective solution was the one that cost only two dollars, I still don't regret buying the high-end Wile E. Coyote Drain Clearer. After all, you can't put a price on entertainment.

# 41

## "COPACABANA" AND OTHER SONGS I'LL DEFEND TO THE DEATH

Music isn't just something I hear in the background while I'm busy doing other stuff. It's the cement that adheres memories to my brain, a time machine that's capable of launching me backwards five, ten, thirty years with just a few notes. My friend Philippa and I recently hosted a live episode of our podcast that featured an acoustic duo called The Sweater Set, and that got us thinking about the songs that make up the soundtrack of our lives. I limited myself to 15, and they appear in no particular order. Don't judge me.

- "Copacabana" by Barry Manilow. I hold my mother completely responsible for this. I grew up hearing Barry croon from the console stereo while Mom cleaned the house. Long before I had any idea what the Merengue or the Cha-Cha looked like, I was well aware of a showgirl named Lola's ability to do them and the fact that those skills somehow got her boyfriend shot. (From this song I inferred that dancing was a life-threatening pursuit, which I think explains my utter failure at ballet as a child. Adult, too, come to think of it.) I picked up Barry's entire repertoire by osmosis, in fact, as did my siblings. My brother and I figured this out as teenagers when we happened to be out somewhere together and "Mandy" began to play. The lyrics came flying out of the two of us automatically and completely by rote, the same way we spoke the Nicene Creed during Sunday Mass.

- "What a Fool Believes," by the Doobie Brothers. This was one of the first singles I purchased, if not the very first. "What a Fool Believes" was a radio staple in 1980, which meant that I heard it several times a week as various moms drove our carpool to and from swim practice in the mornings. I could barely decipher a single word Michael McDonald sang and had no idea what the song was about, but it stuck with me anyway.

- "Through the Years," by Kenny Rogers. It just now occurs to me that, given my affinity for Barry Manilow, the Doobie Brothers, and Kenny Rogers, even as a child I must have known that I was destined to spend large chunks of my life in a dentist's chair. Anyway, when I was eleven, my best friend Liz and I became die-hard Kenny Rogers fans. Do not ask me how or why, because I really have no idea. Liz and I also thought we wanted to become architects, so we would sit in her room, reading *Home* magazine and drawing elaborate floor plans on graph paper while belting out Kenny's greatest hits. "Through the Years" was our pièce de résistance, and we sang it with gusto even though the combined total of years Liz and I had gone through was 22. Our biggest trial and tribulation at that time was probably the fact that we were listening to Kenny Rogers instead of Ozzy Osbourne, like most normal kids our age.

- "Take On Me," by A-ha. The opening riff of this song hooked me the first time I heard it. It earned a permanent spot on my life's soundtrack because of the role it played at a pool party one night during the summer after eighth grade. Earlier in the school year, I had developed a major crush on a very cute drummer named Dave. At the pool party, the gods of adolescent love plopped Dave on the lounge chair next to mine. We talked for most of the night. He seemed Interested in me, a development I regarded as a near-miracle because my head was encased in a full suite of orthodontic armor. The next day, Dave rode his bicycle to my parents' house—a distance of six miles one way—to ask me out on a date. I was stunned, but somehow managed to say "yes." We went on only one date, Dave and I, and it was a double date with my sister and her boyfriend (someone had to drive, after all). He moved on to someone else right away. If love were a bullpen, I had been a mere setup pitcher, but I still claim that episode as a minor triumph. And the braces are off now, Dave. Just sayin'.

• "1999," by Prince. As much as I love nearly all of Prince's music, only this song makes the cut for two reasons. First, I distinctly remember hearing it at the first dance I ever went to, held in the cafeteria of Lake Braddock Secondary School in Burke, Virginia. It was the fall of 1983, and when "1999" came on, I wanted desperately to dance to it. But, like many eighth graders, my dancing shoes were weighed down by a total lack of self-confidence. Instead of dancing, I clung to the cafeteria wall like mold. Sixteen years later, dancing redemption arrived. It was December 31, 1999, and I was ringing in the landmark year at a hotel party in Richmond featuring my favorite band at the time—Pat McGee—and my favorite people both then and now: my best friend and my siblings. Nothing could have kept me from dancing that night.

- "Sweet Child of Mine," by Guns N' Roses. In August of 1999, we celebrated my sister Lynne's 30th birthday at a sports bar in Reston that happened to feature karaoke. My closest friend, Michelle, and my sister's then-boyfriend, now husband, Paul, were also in attendance. Michelle and Paul got along okay but weren't each other's preferred company. Yet, after Lynne and I got booed off the stage for our joint rendition of "I Can't Smile Without You" (by, who else, Barry Manilow), the unlikely duo of Michelle and Paul took the stage and delivered a surprisingly respectable rendition of "Sweet Child of Mine" by Guns 'N' Roses. And just last summer, when Michelle was visiting from Seattle, she and Paul reprised their classic and performed it for my 42nd birthday, only this time with customized lyrics and a title—"Wheat Child of Mine"—that honored my longstanding nickname. Weird Al would have been proud. Axl Rose, perhaps not.

- "Hey, Nineteen," by Steely Dan. This song evokes the best date of my entire life. The date took place in the summer of 2000, not in a fancy restaurant or exotic locale, but on the front porch of my then-boyfriend's house in a small, coastal North Carolina town. The whole thing was completely unplanned. It was late afternoon and he had just opened a bottle of red for us to enjoy on the porch. For background, he put on a mix that skewed heavily towards classic rock. It cycled to "Hey, Nineteen," a song I'd heard a few times but paid little attention to beyond bobbing my head to the beat. For whatever reason, I listened closely to the lyrics that time. I had gotten caught up in the singer's lament about having nothing in common with his nineteen year-old girlfriend—she didn't even know who Aretha Franklin was, which is grounds for dumping all by itself if you ask me—when the instrumental kicked in. It would have been a very generic and thoroughly uneventful instrumental, except that the lead singer busted in and said, with no trace of humor whatsoever, "Skate a little lower now," causing me and my boyfriend to split our sides laughing. We spent the rest of the evening picking through our music, finding lesser-known songs we wanted the other person to hear and delighting in listening and laughing. I don't remember what we had for dinner, if we even had dinner. I just know it was, and still is, the best date I ever had.

- "Gonna Make You Sweat," by C+C Music Factory. This song was released in December of 1990, when I was a second year student at the University of Virginia. No UVA party was complete without it. Since songs weren't quite as disposable then as they are now, I heard "Gonna Make You Sweat" no fewer than 14,932 times between its release and my graduation in 1993. I happened to hear it on satellite radio just this morning while driving to work. The instant I heard the words "Everybody dance now," I was no longer plodding along Route 50; the song had cast me back to the Delta Sig house on Rugby Road, where I used to bust out my best moves even though stale beer constantly threatened to Superglue my shoes to the dance floor.

- "Jump," by Van Halen. The moment I heard the opening synth chords, I loved this song, but that's not why it's on this list. It's here because it reminds me of the summer of 1984, when my brother's Little League all-star baseball team won first the local championships and then the state title before traveling to Florida for a regional tournament. I went with them. "Jump," which started out as one of their warm-up tunes, became their anthem. It became mine as well in 2002, thanks to a friend who put it on a mix tape I listened to while training for the inaugural D.C. Marathon. I ran that race with a Walkman radio—MP3 players were in their infancy and I prefer to acquire technology in its geriatric phase—and, somewhere around Mile 10, the classic rock station just happened to play "Jump," resulting in the fastest one mile split of my race. No matter where I am, what I'm doing or what my mood is, whenever I hear that song, it sends my spirits soaring.

- "Message in a Bottle," by the Police. Sometime in the mid- to late 1990s, my entire family piled into our brown minivan (a major upgrade from the two-tone green giant of a van we used to have) to go to Philadelphia for a funeral. We had barely left my parents' development when my sisters and I asked Dad to tune the radio to the classic rock station. Dad has never found much use for any music that came after 1963, but if we asked him to deliver us from the oldies, he usually gave in. He would tune in our station and then tune us out. On this particular day, we were approaching the Woodrow Wilson Bridge that spans the Potomac River when "Message in a Bottle" came on. My sisters and I sang along until we neared the end of the song, where Sting's only message, bottled or otherwise, is "sending out an SOS." He sings the phrase over and over and over again for about thirty seconds straight. About twenty-five seconds into this loop, my father erupted with, "DON'T THEY KNOW ANY OTHER GODDAMNED WORDS?!? TURN THAT SHIT OFF!" Silence reigned in the car for a moment, and then the all of us passengers exploded with laughter. We got the message loud and clear, Dad! To this day, not a one of us can hear this song without cracking up.

- "You Learn," by Alanis Morissette. I disliked every song on "Jagged Little Pill," Alanis's megahit album, with one exception: "You Learn." I liked the music and the laid-back beat. One afternoon in the summer of 1996, the song was playing on my portable radio at the immigration court where I worked as an interpreter –a euphemism for "clerk who happens to speak Spanish"—when our receptionist buzzed my desk. Someone named Mr. Pearson was waiting to see me, she said. I was grateful for the interruption, because I spent most of my days in that job doing mindless paperwork and reflecting on my life. (At 25, my resume included two degrees I was proud of and one broken engagement that I wasn't. I had waited too long to end the relationship and wasn't honest enough, two things guaranteed to make a bad situation worse. My days were plagued by thoughts that the Universe was going to send me into spinsterhood as punishment for my awful behavior.) I frequently got visitors at the court, and they were almost always lawyers who had questions about their cases. I strode through the door and into the waiting area, where I laid eyes on a very handsome, sandy-haired and blue-eyed lawyer I'd seen in court earlier that day.

"Mr. Pearson?" I said, my optimism surely visible. He nodded and smiled. "How can I help you?" I would have been happy to talk to him about anything, including inane immigration forms.

"Um, I was wondering if you'd want to go to dinner with me," he said. When I regained consciousness, I said yes, and we went on to date for quite a while. After that, "You Learn" became what my sister Suzi referred to as an omen song. Whenever I heard it, good things seemed to follow. The song is so old by now that, if I do hear it in the wild, I'm gonna sprint to the nearest lottery retailer.

- "The Way You Look Tonight," by Frank Sinatra. This song landed itself on my list the night of my grandmother's 75th birthday party in the fall of 1996. Of the many things Nana loved in life, dancing and high heels ranked way up there. I remember her twirling around that night in high heels, an elegant party dress, and perfectly coiffed hair (Nana's hair was always perfect). I can't recall whether she and my father danced to this song, or whether it supplied the background music for the celebratory slide show we put on that night, but it really doesn't matter. I just know that hearing "The Way You Look Tonight" conjures up a vision of Nana, radiant and happy, and that vision always produces a huge smile, along with a few tears.

- "Violin Concerto No. 4 ("Winter"), by Antonio Vivaldi. From 1998-2002, I was working full-time and attending law school at George Mason at night. "Winter" somehow became the one thing capable of motivating me to get off my rear and write a paper. Any time I hear it, I see myself in my one bedroom condo in Alexandria, sitting at the beautiful study desk my parents gave me and typing about springing executory interests or some other arcane legal principle I probably still don't understand, while my cat snoozed obnoxiously on my lap.

- "Love on the Rocks," by Sara Bareilles. A friend of mine gave me "Little Voice," Sara Bareilles's debut album, just before I went on a road trip to the Northern Neck of Virginia in the summer of 2007. I stuck it in the CD player the minute I hit a wide-open stretch of Route 17. I immediately loved the bluesy, piano-heavy backdrop of "Love on the Rocks," but what really hooked me was the line: "Here's a simplification of everything we're going through/You plus me is bad news." As it turns out, I was at that very moment trying to shake off the overtures of a man I was quite attracted to but who was noncommittal and, objectively, not good for me. Sara's equation, and the follow-up line—"my friend says I look better without you"—pretty well summed it up. But hey, I didn't go to law school to get bogged down with annoying math, so I ignored it and learned the hard way instead.

- "Knee Deep," by the Zac Brown Band. When I left my husband in July of 2011, my life was in free fall, but I wasn't. The hands of friends and family reached out by the dozens to catch me before I could even ask, and help came in all sorts of ways. For example, my brother and sister-in-law, who live in Georgia, made their presence felt with music. They sent me a care package that included a mix CD they named "Songs You Love But Are Embarrassed To Admit It." (Clearly they had no idea my CD collection already included "Glam Rock I" and "Glam Rock II: The Glam Strikes Back.") My very favorite song on this hilarious mix is "Knee Deep," which features the lines: "Cause now I'm/Knee deep in the water somewhere/Got the blue sky breeze blowing wind through my hair/Only worry in the world is the tide gonna reach my chair." My mind grabbed those lines and held on to them for dear life, picturing the day when high tide would top my list of cares. Like "Jump," it became an anthem. Whenever I felt like I was faltering, I'd cue up "Knee Deep," smile in the general direction of my future, and keep pressing forward.

# 42

## LETTING GO OF LOVE WHILE HANGING ON FOR DEAR LIFE

F ew things are harder than letting go of a true love. I know, because I just did it.

I was forced a few weeks ago to end a long-term relationship that had been a source of stability and caused me almost no stress. I ended it even though we were both content and there was nothing wrong. It was one of those relationships that couldn't last forever and I had always known that, so I just tried to enjoy what we had while we had it. I had a long time to prepare for the end, but that still didn't make it any easier. You never really know what goodbye will feel like until the moment is upon you.

When the moment came, I felt like sobbing.

KAREN YANKOSKY

Somehow I managed to hold back my tears as I handed the keys to my blue, 2004 six-speed Acura RSX Type-S to my nephew, who had just gotten his learner's permit. I had no idea that letting go would be so hard when I promised the car to J.J. a decade earlier. Promises are funny like that: easy to make when the probability and date of execution both seem remote.

Oh, the places we'd gone, that little blue car and I. It took me to Hilton Head and back to visit a long-distance boyfriend. It helped a dear friend race to the hospital to see his father, who'd just had a stroke. It made trips to fields and gyms across Virginia for various family sporting events. It held my belongings when I decided to leave my husband and the Yuppie Prison in July of 2011. That car was the one thing that felt a little bit normal as the rest of my life was falling apart around me.

When I moved in with my sister and her family that summer, I carted my seven and nine year-old nephew and niece all over the place in my two-door delight. The Roommates sat in the backseat, which was so cramped they couldn't get out unless I pressed a lever that sent the front seat forward a few inches. They soon realized that, if they wrapped their arms around the passenger seat while I pressed the lever, they could shoot forward with the seat, a game they loved. Sometimes I launched them five or six times before we even left the driveway. Once we got going, we would sing pop atrocities like "Dynamite" by Taio Cruz at the top of our lungs. When I think back to that summer, happy memories of these sing-along ride-alongs crowd out the misery of extricating myself from a terrible marriage.

But after ten years, the time had come for me to set my love free.

Just before dusk a few Sundays ago, I drove my eldest nephew to a large, deserted, and hilly church parking lot. After I parked the car and shut off the ignition, we switched places. It took me more than a few minutes to adjust to the view from the passenger seat. As we buckled our seatbelts, I realized I had given no thought whatsoever to how to teach stick shift to J.J. My mind raced back to the two-phase approach that had been used when I learned how to drive stick at age 23.

Phase one had consisted of a very brief lesson administered by my father in the Lake Braddock Secondary School parking lot. After I'd managed to get the car in gear and moving forward exactly twice, Dad pronounced me ready to hit the road. I disproved his pronouncement almost immediately by stalling four times in a row. On a hill. In traffic. After the fourth stall, I came unglued, yanked the emergency brake, stormed out of the car, and yelled, "YOU DRIVE! I'M WALKING HOME!"

Phase two followed a few days later and was led by my nineteen year-old brother. Perhaps because he hadn't expected to find himself in a teaching role, his guidance consisted of one sentence: "It's like walking in slow-motion: as you put your left foot down on the clutch, you lift your right foot off of the gas, and then reverse it." If my brother was short on advice, he was long on patience, so eventually I got it.

At the risk of depriving my nephew of an important educational experience, I decided that we could skip phase one and go straight to phase two. I passed down my brother's one-sentence pearl of wisdom and hoped it would be enough. I felt surprisingly calm, considering that neither J.J. nor I knew what we were doing. Right away, my nephew stalled, as most people do when learning to drive stick. Three or four additional stalls allowed me to diagnose the problem.

"Give it more gas," I said, my Zen state undisturbed. The stalling continued. I tried coaching him while he was in the process of shifting. "Gas," I said once more, calmly. He gave it more juice, but I could tell we were still on the brink. I started to lose my Zen and began to repeat the word, increasing the speed and volume of my speech until I could have passed for a World Cup commentator.

After five solid minutes of "Gas…gas…gas gas gas gas GAS GAS GAS!" J.J. started to get the hang of it. We spent another half hour in the parking lot executing various maneuvers, only a few of which made me lurch in my seat like a cat in the throes of a hairball. I decided we were ready to take on the streets of Arlington.

"Just remember two things, J.J.," I said. "Rule number one: stay calm. Rule number two: gas. Gas gas gas gas gas."

And we were off. For the next forty-five minutes, my nephew drove well, stalling only once and recovering right away. We decided to head back home. I thought we were in the clear until an aggressive driver tailgated and then passed my nephew on a one-lane road a few blocks from my house. J.J. was rattled, which I realized only as he was pulling the car into the driveway. My driveway is a flat surface except for the concrete apron that leads to it. That apron, which rises two inches at its peak, might as well have been Mount Everest. J.J. stalled once. Twice. Three times. After the fourth, I caught a whiff of an unfamiliar odor. It smelled somewhat like formaldehyde, a scent I associate more with funeral homes than driveways. It took me a second to realize the stench emanated from my clutch, which was burning. Suddenly the funeral connection seemed apropos. Tears sprang to my eyes and I resorted to mouth-breathing.

"Oh my GOD, Aunt Wheat. I can't do it," J.J. said, making me fear that we might end up going through phase one after all. I couldn't let it happen. I grabbed the emergency brake and put the car in neutral.

"Don't worry, pal. You're totally okay. I know that guy threw you off, but you did absolutely nothing wrong, except you forgot rule number one. Which is...?"

He let out an exasperated sigh. "Stay calm," he said, only it came out as, "Steh hahm," because his teeth were gritted.

"And rule number two?"

"Gas." He paused for a split second and then said, "Gas gas gas gas GAS GAS GAS!" in his best World Cup announcer voice.

When we stopped laughing, I said, "Okay, give it another shot." This time, he remained calm. And boy, did he ever remember to give it gas. We rocketed into the driveway so fast I thought we might break the sound barrier, or at least the gate to my backyard.

After a hearty laugh and a change of underwear, my nephew and I agreed that, even if we didn't go all that far, we had definitely turned a corner together. And I knew my love was in very good hands.

# ACKNOWLEDGEMENTS

Appearing on the cover of a book with a plunger in hand, like most dreams come true, didn't happen on its own. I had a lot of help, which means I have a lot of thank-yous to distribute.

The first goes to my divorce. Without it, I might not have enrolled in a writing class called "Getting Started" to take my mind off of the misery. The course, led expertly by Dorothy Spruzen, lived up to its name and helped me convert my thoughts of writing to reality. I'll be first in line if Dorothy ever teaches a writing class called "Getting Paid."

If I'm being honest, though, my parents and siblings spent decades pushing me to write. Had they realized how often I would end up writing about them, they might have withheld some of that encouragement. Since it's too late for that, Mom, Dad, Suzi, Lynne and L.J., you're stuck with a crummy "thank you/sorry" at the back of a book. I love you all very much. You're the best team imaginable, and I'm lucky to have a spot on your roster. (Next time, consider holding tryouts.)

To my friend Nick Galifianakis, thanks for reading my chatty emails and saying, "This is your book, right? Please tell me this is your book." It was my book, I just didn't know it. Thanks for nudging me in the right direction, sharing your insights, and believing in my writing.

Speaking of believers, I owe huge debt of gratitude to the Westover Beer Garden. I went there on a beautiful summer night, seeking nothing more than a nice outdoor place to write. I left with a crew of new supporters and friends, as well as an editor. Two WBG patrons, Wayne Heinrichs and Larry Jackson, warrant special mention. Wayne, thanks for being a humor essay with legs. And Larry, thank you for spending hours editing my work and claiming to enjoy every minute of it. You made a difference.

To Ned Hickson, I sincerely appreciate your hilarious writing and also your willingness to risk guilt by association by supporting this project.

To Michelle Foye, you will always be the graphic designer I go to when I want to look my best while holding a plumbing implement. Thank you for your ideas, enthusiasm, and patience. To Laura Conner, thank you for 25 years of friendship and for being the kind of professional who can stop laughing long enough to snap a great picture.

I'd never have reached the point where I found my-self posing for a plunger photo without the support of dear friends like Michelle Speir, Ken Iliffe, Thom Tyler, and Cat and "Oli" Oliver. You read my writing the minute it first appeared online and, even though some of it stunk, you pushed me to keep going.

Thank you to Lauren Rosenblatt, for patiently reading my early drafts and for seeing what my tired eyes could not, and to Victoria Milkovich and Greg Rakes for volunteering so enthusiastically to read my manuscript mid-edit.

To my beloved Smash Hits, thank you for being a wellspring of support and material, and for giving me a chance to pay tribute to Carmela "CeCe" Alves, our dear friend and teammate who passed away just before this went to press. I hope her family is in some way honored by her presence in these pages.

To Paulette Beete and Marcus Dowling, know how grateful I am that you have held my writing in high enough regard to encourage other people to read it.

To Jennifer Tress, thank you for your friendship and for your incredible generosity in mentoring me. Writing a book is a marathon, and when you saw that

I'd hit the wall, you motivated me to keep going and finish strong.

To Philippa Hughes, I give you a great big hug, because you always let me even though you don't really like it. Thank you so much for being my friend, writing partner, fan, co-host, and honest broker, all rolled into one, and for knowing which of those I need on any given day.

And to you, dear reader, thank you for spending this time with me.

# ABOUT THE AUTHOR

A longtime resident of the Washington, D.C., area, Karen Yankosky spends her working hours lawyering. She should make up for that by performing acts of charity and other noble works in her spare time, but instead she fritters it away writing, podcasting, trying to date, and writing and podcasting about trying to date. You can find her writing at www.splatospheric.com and her podcast at www.womenofuncertainage.com. She's @MizYank on Twitter, tweeting with the frequency of a mute bird.